THE
MAINLINER'S SURVIVAL GUIDE
to the
Post-Denominational World

Derek Penwell

CHALICE
PRESS

ST. LOUIS, MISSOURI

Cover design: Elizabeth Wright

www.ChalicePress.com

Print: 9780827223646

EPUB: 978082723653 EPDF: 978082723660

Library of Congress Cataloging-in-Publication Data

Penwell, Derek.
Mainliner's survival guide to the post-denominational world / by Derek Penwell.
—First [edition].
    pages cm
Includes bibliographical references and index.
ISBN 978-0-8272-2364-6 (pbk. : alk. paper)
1. United States—Church history. 2. Christianity—21st century. I. Title.

BR515.P46 2014
277.3'08--dc23   2014022987

Printed in the United States of America

Contents

Introduction: The Vortex of Doom   1

SECTION 1—WHERE WE CAME FROM

1 Religion after the Revolutionary War   15

2 Stone-Campbell and the Seeds of Reform   26

3 What Can We Learn?   37

SECTION 2—HOW WE'RE CONTINUING OUR LEGACY

4 "Spiritual but Not Religious" or Missional Rather   54
   Than Institutional

5 "Everybody's Welcome Here" or Theologically Inclusive   80

6 "Just a Minute, I Have to Update My Status" or   97
   Technologically Savvy

SECTION 3—HOW CAN WE CONTINUE MOVING INTO A POST-DENOMINATIONAL WORLD?

7 "I Like Jesus; It's His Followers I Can't Stand" or Jesus the   117
   Social Radical

8 "Are We Meeting at the Coffee House or the Pub?" or the   139
   Church as Radical Community

9 "Going Green ... All the Cool Kids Are Doing It" or   157
   Ecologically Concerned

10 "How About, You Know ... the Gays?"   167

Conclusion   185

Bibliography   187

Introduction
The Vortex of Doom

In my first church out of seminary, I found myself in the coal country of Southeastern Kentucky. The coal industry, by the time I arrived, had experienced a serious decline. As a result, large numbers of people had migrated to other parts of the country in search of work. The cities and towns of Appalachia were beleaguered; and the city I came to was no exception. In fact, it was the poster child for the ravages of decline.

Not long after I arrived, I picked up the local newspaper only to read the headline that, according to the latest census, my new city had the dubious distinction of being identified as the fastest declining city in the Commonwealth of Kentucky. At the same time, there arose great handwringing in my denomination, the Christian Church (Disciples of Christ), over the news that we were the fastest declining denomination in American religious life.

The church I was to pastor had its own problems. A once-proud downtown mainline Protestant church, it had gotten grayer and grayer. At one point we went eighteen months without church school for anyone under the age of eighteen. Things looked dire. For a young minister fresh out of seminary, it felt like someone had handed me the wheel of the Titanic as it was sinking into the deep.

I had just been on the job a few days when Lorraine came into my office and said, "Preacher, you've come here to bury us."

"I hope not, Lorraine." But what I was thinking was, "I can't afford for my first church to go belly up. That won't be a career enhancer."

I felt mounting anxiety about the prospect of failure. I kept hearing variations on the same theme: "We'd better get some young people in here, or we're going to die." Inevitably these comments came from well-meaning people who remembered a time when First Christian bustled with activity, when even the wrap-around balcony was full and "You couldn't swing a dead cat in church without hitting a child." This is one of the reasons they sought a young minister: They thought that maybe a young minister could attract some young families.

Fear of death hung in the air. But while things looked grim, I began having nagging doubts about my own disquiet. *Why,* I wondered to myself, *should we continually focus on what's wrong with us?* We didn't make the local economy. We didn't cause the denominational contraction. In many ways, we didn't even have a lot of control over what happened to the drop in membership in our own congregation—young people graduated and moved away in search of jobs, and the downtown suffered as businesses relocated out on the highway. We found ourselves in a cycle of panic and diminished hope that I referred to as the *vortex of doom*—that situation in which negativity builds on itself, causing a downward spiral.

The vortex of doom threatened to consume us. It lay as a subtext beneath every conversation, and lurked on the periphery of every meeting as an unwanted guest. Our eyes betrayed our apprehension of what, we felt certain, awaited us in the future. I knew I couldn't join in the public rehearsal of our anxieties, but in private I was just as afraid as everyone else that the whole thing would go belly up, and that I'd be left to explain how I took a historic one-hundred-year-old congregation and ran it into the ground.

So I started preaching about hope. I took every opportunity to say that we served a God of resurrection, a God *used* to raising the dead. I received a lot of polite smiles for my efforts. But I could tell that people were only attempting to save me from my mounting discouragement without releasing the grip on their own.

I realize now how difficult it must have been for them to try to protect me from the corrosiveness of the despair that had settled on us. Seeing a different future from the one that threatens to undo you takes a robust imagination—and the first casualty of despair is imaginative thinking.

Then one day, after reading about how a cancer patient in hospice care began to take trips she thought she would never take and try things she'd never had the courage to try, it struck me: The prospect of death need not necessarily imprison us; it could, if we were able to shift our thinking, *liberate* us. It could free us from the burden of our own expectations about what churches are supposed to look like, and let us live whatever life we had left with holy abandon.

At a particularly grim elders' meeting, after I announced that we wouldn't be hosting a vacation Bible school that summer because we had neither the children nor the volunteers, someone started wondering out loud again about how much longer we were going to be around.

I finally got tired of all the fear and anxiety. I said, "Here are a few Bibles. Look toward the back at Paul's letters. Do you see all of those churches? Ephesus. Philippi. Colossae. Do you know what they're up to nowadays? Heard any inspiring stories about new family life centers at First Church Philippi? Anything about new soup kitchens at First Church Colossae? Any rumors about bold new youth ministry models at First Church Ephesus?"

Silence. Then someone spoke up and said, "I don't even know if any of those churches are still around."

Channeling acerbic theologian Stanley Hauerwas, I said, "Exactly. So, let's concede that God has killed off better churches than we're ever going to be, and quit worrying about it. Instead of fretting over whether we're heading for the junk heap, why don't we just put the pedal down and see what this old thing can do. If it blows up, well, it was on its way out anyway. If it catches life, though, just think what God could do with it. But the point is that this is God's church, not ours. Why don't we start concentrating on the work of faithful ministry, and let God worry about where the finish line is?"

I'd love to be able to say that things took a sharp turn toward the better after that elders meeting, but I wouldn't be telling the truth. The truth is that it took a while. Handwringing is a habit that takes time and practice to cultivate. Learning to let go of anxiety is also a habit, one I fear the church has taken very little initiative to foster. And though congregations, which generally operate with a thinner margin for error, are especially prone to despondency, denominations can also find themselves fainthearted about the future. Protestant mainline denominations, in particular, have fallen on hard times over the last generation, with denominations slipping into their own vortex of doom.

Are We Even Going to Be Around in Ten Years?

Get together with a group of mainline ministers and sooner or later somebody is going to say, "I'm not even sure our denomination is going to be here in ten years." I'm not sure why the event horizon is always a round number, nor am I sure what ecclesiastical tea leaves help generate this number, but it seems to be a mathematical constant.

"Ten years? Are you sure about the number?"

"Well, you know what I mean. Sooner rather than later."

Mainline denominations typically occupy the center of discussion about decline—particularly decline in church membership. For years it was argued that the trends indicated that liberal theology was to blame, driving members away. But lately, even more theologically conservative churches have experienced a decline in membership. The Southern Baptist Convention, a widely conservative denomination characterized by consistent growth during the period of the mainline membership slump, has just posted a third year of declining membership numbers.[1] The latest figures for 2010 indicate that church membership across the board in the SBC has fallen off by 1.05%.

My own denomination, the Christian Church (Disciples of Christ), has flailed about in uncertain waters for years. Since 1968, when the Christian Church restructured, officially becoming a denomination, it has lost 901,449 members (57%) and over 2,108 congregations (36%). By comparison, between 1965 and 2005, the United Church of Christ lost (41%) of its members, while the Presbyterian Church (USA) lost 46%. And though since 2006 the decline among Disciples has slowed considerably, losing only 1% of its members and .5% of its congregations, the continued downward trend has many Disciples worried about the long-term viability of the denomination.

Let's be honest, the statistical trend is frightening. Last year alone, membership figures for mainline denominations were down across the board: United Methodist Church (-1.01%), Evangelical Lutheran Church in America (-1.96%), Presbyterian Church (U.S.A.) (-2.61%), Episcopal Church (-2.48%), American Baptist Church (-1.55%), United Church of Christ (-2.83%).[2] Sadly, when I go to Google and type in "mainline denomination," the first suggestion Google provides is "mainline denomination decline."

Despite that bracing picture, however, I want to suggest that mainline denominations have great reason for hopefulness. Considering the religious climate of the post-Revolutionary War period, which produced or amplified the importance of certain mainline denominations like the Methodists and the Disciples, we may see similarities with our own post-denominational world that offer a different way from the well-worn path that leads down the vortex of doom. By looking to the expansion of religion in America during the post-Revolutionary War period, I will argue that we can begin to see how mainline denominations might find strength in some of the historic theological, ecclesiological, and even technological innovations taken up during that religiously desperate period to help negotiate an uncertain future.

---

[1] Statistics from (http://www.ncccusa.org/news/110210yearbook2011.html.

[2] African American churches that might be considered mainline denominations (AME, AME Zion, and CME) do not report membership data, according to the National Council of Churches.

"Yeah, but are we going to be around in ten years?"

My point is: I don't even think that's the right way to think about it. If all we've got is ten years, then let's use the time to do things that are so radical, so amazingly unthinkable that after ten years we'll all be either so energized that we want to sign up for another tour, or so exhausted that we'll all keel over and won't have to worry about it anymore.

Mainline denominations are dying. If the trends hold true, as they have over the past forty years, we're careening toward a post-denominational world—a world in which the structures that supported progressive theology, a social justice orientation toward faith, and institutionalized mission and administration is crumbling before our eyes; a world in which the printed media that has supported denominational ministry (publishing houses, curricula, magazines, journals, etc.)—over which denominations could exert control—is being overtaken by electronic media (ePub, blogging, social media)—over which denominations exert only minimal control; a world in which mainline cultural ascendancy and domination isn't only a relic of the past, but no longer even a desirable goal for the future.

The purpose of this book, however, is not to lead cheers for the death of mainline denominationalism. But neither is the purpose to help mainline denominations hang onto dying systems just a little bit longer. My purpose is to help mainline denominations and their congregations get a correct read on the situation, embrace death as a liberation from having to "succeed," and learn how to live.

After all, the gospel is first about failure and death—because it's only losers and corpses who've got nothing left to lose. Why a people who remember the failure of the crucifixion and celebrate the victory of resurrection in the Eucharist every Sunday should have its sphincter seize up every time it thinks of death is beyond me.

Embrace failure as a road to success—even God did.

The Seeds of Hope in an Emerging World

A tendency to foster the democratically governed local church and to discount or oppose hierarchies and higher judicatories of the church, a concern for practical achievements rather than doctrinal purity, and a pervasive and growing disinclination for formalism in worship, intellectualism in theology, and otherworldly conceptions of piety and morality. (Ahlstrom, 382)

To my mind, this quote captures the essence of American religious life over the past 40 to 50 years. Since the radical upheavals of the 1960s, American society in general and the church in particular have faced the reality of a growing distrust in institutional authority, an impulse to seek truth in personal experience rather than in received orthodoxies, and a move away from the settled and the traditional toward what is considered novel, and therefore, authentic. Increasingly, the church finds people seeking less for reliable doctrine than for authentic practice, for ways of living that take the present seriously without putting everything on hold until some eschatological future.

"That's us, right?"

Interestingly, the time period Sydney Ahlstrom refers to isn't twenty-first century America but the period just after the Revolutionary War—the period that gave birth to the Second Great Awakening and the explosion of denominational strength among a few daring religious pioneers who ventured into the uncertain frontiers of the new American West.

The similarities between the revolutionary era and the post-denominational world we live in are striking. Ahlstrom writes, "The revolutionary era was a period of decline for American Christianity as a whole. The churches reached a lower ebb of vitality during the two decades after the end of hostilities than at any other time in the country's religious history" (Ahlstrom, 365). Contrary to the popular picture of the Revolutionary era as a time marked by the religious fervor that drove the pilgrims to seek a new setting in which to practice their faith freely, the time following the Revolutionary War saw great apathy toward religion and a significant deterioration of the institutional church. Because of its part in helping to underwrite the imperial politics of Britain, the institutional church labored under the suspicions of the newly liberated colonials. People regularly equated ecclesiastical authority with the imperial authority against which the revolutionaries had fought. Kings and bishops sparked many of the same feelings in colonial America.

"Kings. Bishops. Ah, they're all fancy. We're tired of fancy. That's why we came here."

A new sense of freedom arose during the post-Revolutionary War period. The realization of the "freedom *from* religion" became a compelling narrative. People, used to established religion into which everyone was born, found themselves not only free to choose among a variety of religious expressions but free to choose *no* religious expression at all.

Liberated from the politically imperial pretensions of the old world, people also began to understand themselves as liberated from the religiously imperial pretensions of that same world. Simply put, the idea that external forces could no longer control people in the ways they were accustomed to being controlled was intoxicating. Like an eighteen-year-old college freshman who's been made to go to church her whole life and wakes up on her first Sunday away from home, rubs her eyes, and says, "Screw it. I'm going back to sleep."

Moreover, in the aftermath of the Revolutionary War, many more people began to leave the familiarity of home and move westward, exploring new frontiers and settling unknown lands. As a practical matter, this exploration of new frontiers took them farther and farther from the reaches of the established centers of ecclesiastical authority. The considerable influence of the church in the East all but disappeared as the pioneers moved further westward. Few prelates or pastors were looking over their shoulders.

Due to a number of factors that I will discuss in chapter 1, the overwhelming majority of people spurned membership in the church. But for those who retained religious commitments, geographic distance from the clergy-dominated institutional church produced a desire among the laity for greater input into religious life. People, even really devout, don't-rock-the-boat, preachers-shouldn't-have-long-hair-and-tattoos kind of people, wanted more say in religious life.

By nature the pioneers—who were formed in the heady political and philosophical environment prompted by the founding of a new country on modern Enlightenment ideals, and who daily dealt with the rigors of life on the frontier—tended not to be acquiescent. They were, in other words, Chuck Norris. It should be no surprise, then, that the necessarily self-sufficient pioneers began to express reluctance to submitting to authority, even ecclesiastical authority.

By now, the sentiments about the religious climate of the post-Revolutionary War era ought to sound familiar to contemporary ears. Over the past fifty years people have grown progressively apathetic about the maintenance of American religious institutions—especially Protestant mainline denominations. Given the popular emphasis in the news on mega-churches, struggling mainline denominations can't help but sound like either quaint religious boutiques or ecclesiastical retirement communities where everyone wears brown polyester and white socks. Ironically, this apathy stems, at least in part, from the institutional success of those denominations in the aftermath of World War II and the rebuilding of the American economy during the Cold War. Mainliners came to see themselves as culturally relevant because of their dedication to the stewardship of American institutions and ideals. They "liked Ike" and voted reliably Republican.

Churches had a prominent place in helping the country recover from the economic and social depredations of the Great Depression, the dislocation of the war, and the moral peril posed by Nazism and its "Final Solution." After years of uncertainty America required a massive effort to restore its economic, political, and cultural confidence, and mainline churches gladly filled the role of cheerleader. Mainline denominations became something like a sanctified auxiliary of the U.S. Chamber of Commerce.

The underwriting of American ideals worked initially for the mainline churches. People flocked to them. Membership roles swelled. Clergy were viewed as priests of a common civil religion that held basic expectations of a moral sense of fairness, capitalist progress, and patriotic duty. Mainline churches helped to heal the wounds of a nation that had seen great hardship; but they also amplified the American sense of its expanding role as the political and industrial leader in the battle against the new threat of Communism. However, the success of mainline denominations also planted the seeds for the present crisis. Because mainline denominations had so closely aligned themselves with the post-war American democratic politics and capitalist economics, American religious institutions found themselves being questioned alongside their political and economic counterparts during the cultural upheaval of the 1960s. To many in the countercultural movement, the American Protestant mainline was no less established than was the Church of England in the eyes of the colonials, and it was regarded with no less suspicion than its Anglican counterparts 175 years before. As ecclesiastical authorities had been seen to be collaborators in British imperialism in the Revolutionary era, ecclesiastical authorities in the Cold War era came to be seen as collaborators in what many took to be American imperial pretensions.

As in the aftermath of the Revolutionary War, the 1960s brought with it what amounted to at the time as the radical idea of the "freedom *from* religion." That people felt freer to choose *no* religion in the 1960s was not a newly discovered option; atheism had already existed as a novel practice among the intelligentsia (though as a highly suspect undertaking). Nevertheless, in a country that had largely assumed a form of American civil religion, which was vaguely Christian in its moral leanings and explicitly friendly to religious institutions, the idea that one could choose to opt out of religion altogether once again proved intoxicating. The 1960s were characterized by a cultural shift from institutional-religion-as-a-necessary-good to institutional-religion-as-necessarily-questionable. There were, of course, exceptions to the wide cultural distrust of religion, most notably the Civil Rights movement. But more and more, institutional religion came to be conflated with traditional American political and cultural institutions, all of which were viewed with greater suspicion. Mainline denominations were an appendage of "the man" that American youth were busy "stickin' it to."

Furthermore, in the same way the early Americans pushed westward into unknown frontiers, settling new and unknown lands, contemporary Americans have also found themselves at the edge of vast new frontiers, driven largely by technology. Over the past fifty years American ingenuity has allowed us to explore previously unimagined frontiers. Our fascination with space, for instance, has resulted in trips to the moon, as well as unmanned explorations into the deepest reaches of our solar system. We've pressed the limits of knowledge all the way to cosmic levels, staking out new boundaries for human investigation.

Not only have new vistas of outer space opened up, but so have the seemingly infinite expanses of inner space. Our own bodies have proven to be an especially interesting focus of our colonizing tendencies. We now understand in very intimate ways how our bodies operate, using amazingly sophisticated diagnostic mapping tools—CT scans, MRI, sonography; not to mention the varieties of endoscopy, arthroscopy, and laparoscopy. Technology has provided volumes of new information, even down to the most basic genetic levels, through genomic mapping. With the advances in targeted Pharmacology and Nanotechnology, there is rising optimism about our eventual abilities to subdue and master our bodies (www.nanotechproject. org/inventories/medicine).

And perhaps just as importantly, our exploration of the new frontiers of cyberspace has come to characterize our modern self-understanding as autonomous agents bound together with others only by ties we choose.[3] Daily, Americans run private expeditions to the furthest reaches of cyberspace. And through social media like Facebook, Twitter, and YouTube, people are able to form social and communal bonds.

However, instead of being social ties and communal relationships inherited through the vagaries of birth and family connection, these new communities

[3]Who says "cyberspace" anymore? I know. Using the term "cyberspace" is dated. But, for my purposes, it does help me extend the geographic/spatial metaphor. So, just bear with me, hipster.

center on the choices of the individual. Instead of spending one's life in a particular place, bound to particular institutions, people are both more mobile and less constrained by traditional connections.

Young people, if they have faith commitments at all, feel diminishing loyalties to the denominations in which they grew up. The freedom to blaze one's own trail provided by the Internet symbolizes the amazing array of options available to people in other aspects of their lives. With virtually all facets of life set before us like an endless buffet line in which we are encouraged to take what we want and ignore the rest, the mainline church, with its presumed investment in established institutional structures and hierarchies, has often found the contemporary world not especially hungry for what it's serving.

Although the attitudes toward mainline denominations today often seem depressingly bleak, like our forebears in the revolutionary era, there is great cause for hope. For the barren religious soil found in the wake of the Revolutionary War was the same soil from which sprouted the Second Great Awakening, energizing the remarkable growth of Christianity in America. As the nineteenth century dawned, religious enthusiasm had begun to take hold on the frontier. Through the phenomenon of revivals, people who had previously walked away from established churches rediscovered the church in new and transformative ways. The Second Great Awakening prompted a revolutionary impulse to egalitarianism, a renewed sense of the missionary nature of the gospel, and a growing concern for the pursuit of social justice. Moreover, the expansion of denominations, fueled by the reawakening of religious passion, was viewed positively as an expression of the possibilities of Christian unity within diversity. These same factors, which characterized the flourishing of Christianity in America as a result of the Second Great Awakening, are also present as motivating forces within contemporary Emergence Christianity—that is, the portion of Christianity interested in exploring ways to minister to emerging generations.

In this book I will argue that many of the issues that have historically challenged the established church are, ironically enough, the same issues that have the potential to appeal to those generations of young people who've left the church and to reinvigorate the older generations' sense of mission. Those in the emerging generations—which is to say, Generation X, Generation Y, Millennials, etc.—like those passionate souls of the Second Great Awakening, find vitality in equality, mission, and social justice. They seek an expansive and welcoming community as a more authentic expression of the vision of the Jesus they read about in the Gospels. They also share with their religious ancestors a radical distrust of established religious institutions, as well as a commitment to the exploration of new frontiers.

The Emergence conversation in American Christianity, which takes seriously the concerns of the emerging generations, has risen largely because of the experience of disaffected evangelicals, who have grown tired of what they consider to be the shallowness of popular Evangelicalism—that is (from their perspective), overly reductive theology, doctrine that excludes the "other," slickly packaged too-glib liturgy, and an emphasis on the soul of the individual rather than on the life of the community. However, many of the concerns expressed by emerging Christians resonate with traditional mainline concerns—namely, equality, mission, social justice, and an embrace of diversity. Mainliners have been beating these drums for years, if lately to smaller and smaller audiences.

Why, then, have mainline communities failed to swell with hoards of coffee-drinking tattooed young people? It has, at least in part, to do with some things that emerging Christians share with their ancestors in the Second Great Awakening, but which have often been viewed as threats to a cherished status quo by Mainliners: an active distrust of established institutional structures and an adventurous spirit when it comes to the exploration of new frontiers—in particular, cyberspace and social media.

A Roadmap to the New Frontier

The first section of the book will set the context for a historical comparison between the Second Great Awakening and Emergence Christianity. Chapter 1 will tell the story of the difficulties faced by the church in the wake of the Revolutionary War. This time period saw the church pushed to the margins, struggling to find a voice to speak to people who had lost confidence that the church spoke for anything more than the interests of the socially and politically established. Newfound interest in science and political thought took center stage over more traditionally religious ways of construing the world, rendering the church irrelevant for many people (while for others, it was seen as the core of the problem).

Chapter 2 will then briefly survey the historical and theological impulses that motivated the formation of a particular religious movement that challenged long-held beliefs about what kinds of things people who follow Jesus ought to focus on, as well as how those people ought to organize themselves. The Disciples of Christ and the Methodists, eventual mainline denominations, flourished in many ways as a reaction against the theological and ecclesiological inclinations of institutional churches. The possibilities for how the original concerns motivating the religious explosion prompted by the Second Great Awakening can reenergize contemporary mainline denominations, as well as a description of the fears and desires about the church expressed by emerging generations, will be the subject of chapter 3.

The second section will emphasize the extent to which many of the earliest tendencies of pioneering religious movements after the Second Great Awakening are central features of the Emerging conversation. That is to say, I will argue that mainline denominations, in many cases, can find their place in the religious discussion of emerging generations, not by a total radical discontinuity with their historic theological commitments, but by discovering an intensified continuity with some of the commitments that animated religious growth two hundred years ago. Chapter 4, then, will explore how the skepticism about institutional religious structures can be viewed, not as a threat, but as an opportunity to embrace the passion people have for doing the meaningful work associated with following Jesus. Instead of heavy investments in maintaining organizational structures, emerging generations find energy in mission, and in social justice—a bias they share with many of their mainline denominational forbearers.

Emerging generations also share a commitment to theological inclusivity. Having been raised in a post-denominational world, they have little denominational loyalty. As postmoderns, they are suspicious of univer-salizing meta-narratives that impose orthodoxies. They're ecumenical by temperament, even if not necessarily by informed theological conviction. One of the motivating ideas behind the founding of the Disciples of Christ, for example, was the belief that Christians ought to seek unity as essential to Christian identity. Now, however, emerging generations have pushed beyond the institutional ecumenism that sustained mainline denominations through the last half of the twentieth century to a dawning awareness that they live in a religiously pluralistic world. Chapter 5 will examine ways in which mainliners can take advantage of their historic commitments to unity in the midst of diversity and a radical hospitality that seeks embrace instead of exclusion to meet emerging generations where they are.

Mainline denominations have some historical familiarity with finding their voices on the expanding frontiers of the just recently established United States. The Methodists, with the tradition of the circuit riders, and the Disciples of Christ, with their early ties to frontier revivalism, saw opportunity in the expanding unsettled territories to the west. Envisioning themselves as pioneers, some eventual mainline denominations exerted considerable energy in finding new audiences for the gospel by traveling to where the people were. Moreover, the pioneering spirit evinced a willingness to adapt and use the most effective cultural means to communicate. Chapter 6 will assess the ways that the early use of such tools of communication as the public debate and the printing press provided early mainliners with an opportunity to connect with a massive audience, and how this use of the dominant means of communication resonates in the almost pervasive use of blogging and social media by emerging generations. By rediscovering the innovative spirit that inspired the forebears of mainline denominations to launch expeditions into unknown territories with the most effective tools of communication, it is possible for contemporary Protestant churches to begin to see the bleak and inhospitable future of decline as an adventure, an unexplored but potentially fruitful opportunity to communicate the gospel yet again to new audiences.

Section three will offer three new areas that were not necessarily the historical concerns of early American Christian pioneers, but which can be seen as consistent with their concern to embody the gospel in new and compelling ways to the world in which they lived. Emerging generations, even those who don't care anything about the church, find the Jesus of the Gospels a compelling figure, whose teachings and example hold great potential for a meaningful life lived in a more just and peaceable world. To the extent that emerging generations have given up on the church, for many it has to do with the fact that they can no longer find the Jesus they read about in the Gospels in the teachings and example of his followers. Chapter 7 will consider how mainline denominations can rediscover the radical Jesus of the Gospels, who calls into question the current arrangements guarded by the powers and principalities, and offers a vision of a non-violent world organized equitably to look after the interests of the powerless.

Chapter 8 explores the desire for community among emerging generations. Due to increased mobility and marrying later in life, young people find it more difficult to discover a community that provides meaningful interaction with others. Since some of the traditional ways young people make and sustain friendships are often no longer available to them, emerging generations are seeking communities to connect to. Churches, which are called to be communities where meaningful interactions can occur, have an opportunity to be a place where emerging generations can find the loving embrace of people committed to one another in the service of God.

Another growing concern of emerging generations is stewardship of the planet. They are concerned with issues around the protection of the environment, alternative fuels, and food sustainability. To many among the emerging generations, these are not only practical questions about economic impact, but also moral questions that go to the very heart of our human purpose and destiny. Mainline denominations, which have displayed some sympathies for these concerns, have the potential to offer leadership by helping people think through the moral and theological implications of how we care for God's creation, and why, beyond self-preservation, we might want to do so in the first place.

Finally, I'll take a look at a contemporary reality that those Christians at the turn of the nineteenth century could never have envisioned: the treatment of gay and lesbian people. In chapter 10, I'll spend some time laying out the case that if mainline denominations—which statistically already contain a majority of people in favor of acceptance of homosexuality—want to become a legitimate point of access to Christianity for emerging generations, they're going to have to begin saying so publicly . . . loudly . . . convincingly.

Times are tough for churches—especially mainline churches. The key to survival, though, lies in having confidence that God doesn't need much to accomplish God's purposes. As Martin Luther said, "God can ride the lame horse and shoot the crooked bow." This survival guide seeks to give churches in mainline denominations hope during difficult times by pointing them to familiar aspects of part of their own historical DNA, which have the potential to address concerns shared by emerging generations. (Note: And since it's a survival guide, I've included *Field Notes* with some helpful ideas.) I'm not suggesting a new marketing strategy or a new programmatic initiative that we can sell. Emerging generations have been marketed to death and are instantly skeptical of pre-packaged programs. Instead, learning how to endure in these times will require that the church rediscover and embrace those animating impulses that gave mainline denominations life in the first place. If mainline denominations can manage that, they will have many new partners in the big adventure called "God's future." And if not, they'll die—or at least their current forms will.

1

Religion after the Revolutionary War

The New World Really Is New

"The American Revolution is the most crucial event in American history. The generation overshadowed by it and its counterpart in France stands at the fault line that separates an older world, premised on standards of deference, patronage, and ordered succession, from a newer one that continues to shape our values."

—Nathan O. Hatch

Here's the scene:

The War for Independence has ended. Of course, that doesn't mean everything has returned to normal. In fact, there's a sense in the air that whatever used to pass for "normal" prior to the war can never be recovered—even by those who have a stake in such a world. For one thing, monarchy—the idea that someone set apart by no greater virtue than having had the good sense to have been born to proper parents has the right to control everyone else's lives—is dead, or if not dead, then moribund. The colonies need no longer look to a king or queen to know how they ought to organize their social and political life. They have carved out of the rugged wilderness of the New World a new kind of republic where people selected by the population and not by bloodline govern; they don't rule.

A radical shift in people's everyday orientation to the world has taken place. There have been revolutions in the past. Just over one hundred years before, England had formed a republic, a Commonwealth. The English Civil War had been a terribly bloody and vicious affair, prompting Thomas Hobbes to write the seminal work, *Leviathan*, calling for a social contract that would protect people from the bloody earnestness he believed characterizes people's social behavior when left too long in the play room with a limited number of toys. Though the English revolution led by Cromwell proved that it was possible to call into question the divine right of the monarchy, it didn't entirely do away with the assumption that power ought to be wielded by a certain class of people with superior breeding. At the time of the American Revolution, the idea that people can successfully govern themselves without benefit of a divinely appointed, but often heavy-handed, authority is an earth-shatteringly remarkable idea.

"What? You mean no fancy-pants king gets to tell us how to live anymore?"

Something like that, yes.

Democracy, though it had been known conceptually since the Greeks, becomes a practical reality, as people begin to see themselves as participating members in their own social and political organization.[1] But perhaps more importantly, the *idea* of democracy becomes a metaphor for one's relationship to authority. That is to say, the heady ideals of freedom and liberty that motivated people to take up arms against the tyranny of King George prompt people to begin to question all external authority. "Who are you to tell me to …?"—the time-honored response of adolescents to adult authority—begins to take root as a cultural and intellectual reaction to *any* authority imposed and not self-selected by the individual.

Moreover, not only does the monarchy, the political center of the universe, experience a radical alteration, but the idea of aristocratic classes of people a step down the social and political ladder from royalty occupying privileged positions also falls on hard times. Common assumptions about social class meet with new skepticism, a skepticism that prompts people to begin questioning their understanding of how society ought to be organized. Where before class considerations had carved up the populace into the

---

[1]This new reality, present after the Revolutionary War, isn't Shangri-La, of course. Women and nonAnglos are still considered inferior to their white male counterparts, remaining practically disadvantaged within social, political, and religious hierarchies–even though the idea of hierarchy takes a beating.

power equivalent of the "haves" and the "have-nots," democracy promises to change that.

Fascination with democratic organization causes great excitement by challenging the received tradition about what it means to be born as a part of a classist food chain. Problems arise, according to Hatch, around altogether new issues: "Common folk not respecting their betters, organized factions speaking and writing against civil authority, the uncoupling of church and state, and the abandonment of settled communities in droves by people seeking a stake in the back country" (Hatch, 1989, 6).

"So, bewigged dandies aren't any more important than the rest of us?"

Pretty much, yeah.

What's more, the questioning of traditional ideas leads people to stop and wonder: "Since class and custom have always determined who's in charge, if those criteria are discredited, then who gets to be the boss?" Religion, traditionally a stable force in society, begins to experience upheaval when the masses start questioning the legitimacy of its leaders to lead. Clergy, which had historically been associated with the power of the state, comes to be associated with political hierarchies as a baptized representative of state power. And if you're going to start kicking over government lemonade stands, one of the first things to get muddied is going to be state-sponsored clerics, whose legitimacy comes as much from state sponsorship as from ecclesiastical credentialing. This new democratic suspicion of authority, and the organization that accompanies that authority, bleeds over into people's suspicion of the established clergy. Upstart evangelists and theological entrepreneurs gain popularity, in many cases not in spite of, but because of, their absence from the traditional ecclesiastical pecking order.

"So, you don't need a seminary education, an ordination certificate, or a fancy black robe to be a preacher?"

That about sums it up, yes.

But this upheaval about who gets to call the shots isn't altogether new. The questioning of authority—expressed with deadly enthusiasm in the American Revolution, and rehearsed once again soon after in the French Revolution—has been taking shape for some time under the intellectual banner of the Enlightenment. To get a sense of the intellectual atmosphere that leads to the theological and ecclesiastical ferment of the Second Great Awakening, it is to the Enlightenment we must turn.

Think for Yourself!

The American nation was born in the full illumination of the Enlightenment, and this fact would permanently distinguish it from every other major power in the world.

—SYDNEY AHLSTROM (362)

The Enlightenment, an important period of development in the intellectual history of the West, was in many ways a reaction to the church's claims about what we can know and just who's in the best position to know it. For years, the Catholic Church in Europe held a monopoly on knowledge; which knowledge it maintained must always pass through the filter of faith.

Galileo: The earth revolves around the sun.

The Inquisition: Does not. It says so in the book: "The Lord is king, he is robed in majesty; the Lord is robed, he is girded with strength. He has established the world; it shall never be moved"(Psalm 93:1).

Galileo: It most certainly does, too! I have observed the heavens through a telescope. Science calls into question many of the things we've long held dear.

The Inquisition: If science contradicts Scripture, though, it cannot be true. Correct?

Galileo: Well …

The Inquisition: Perhaps, if you are unpersuaded, we might spend some time working out the kinks in your inadequate understanding of creation.

Galileo: Jeez! You know, now that you mention it, I think my kids *were* goofing around with the equipment. Kids .., right? They eat donuts, then they get the blueberry filling all over the lens. The wife's supposed to keep them out of my stuff, but, I mean, you know how *that* goes, right?

The Inquisition: We knew you'd see things our way.

As the results of the scientific method began to produce a clearer picture of the world, pressure mounted. The Catholic Church's intransigence on the issue of its own position as the locus of intellectual authority continued to erode, issuing in calls for knowledge to be first and foremost a product of reason and not of faith.

Moreover, the displacement of the authority of faith by the authority of reason in the Enlightenment had implications beyond purely scientific knowledge. What about the knowledge required to make moral decisions?

This is no small question. Morality, prior to this time, had been the church's jurisdiction. As the Enlightenment heated up, there were calls to let reason ransom morality from the stranglehold of the church.

In his famous essay "What Is Enlightenment?" Immanuel Kant argues that enlightenment is humanity's attempt to liberate itself from its "self-incurred tutelage" (3). That is to say, for Kant, humanity's moral failure consists in its convention of continuing to take direction from some external authority, rather than, in modern terms, taking the initiative to "think for yourself." Consequently, according to Kant, the remedy for this rational timidity lies in enlightenment—*Sapere aude!*—the determination to trust your own reason. The emphasis for Kant, and for his intellectual heirs in the Enlightenment, is on *your* own reason.

The Church: Pardon us, but you can't do that.

Individual: Says who?

The Church: God does. Wait, we do. Same difference.

Individual: But it seems perfectly reasonable to me.

The Church: It may *seem* perfectly reasonable to do it, but it's not. You're just going to have to trust us on this.

Individual: Why? I can do it if I want to. It's a free country.

The Church: Actually it's not.

Individual: Well, I'm going to *live* like it is.

An epistemological (i.e., locating the final authority for determining what we can know) shift takes place. No longer does knowledge come from faith in what the church *claims* to be true, but from what the individual *decides* to be true based on science. Understandably, this shift in how we know what we know leads to a crisis in the church concerning the way things have always been known.

At the same time, a moral (i.e., locating the final authority for determining what we should do) shift is underway. No longer does church doctrine have the final say in how people ought to live, but individuals begin to take on responsibility as free moral agents. Again, this shift in how we know what we ought to do leads to another crisis in the church.

Knowledge and morality slowly become matters decided not ecclesiastically but individually. In both respects, the church takes a beating at the hands of the Enlightenment.

After the Revolutionary War—a war sustained by Enlightenment ideals— the world in which people live their everyday lives is as radically different a place from what came before it as anything since the Golden Age of Athens. Politics are different. The social order is different. Everything feels different. Even (perhaps, especially) religion. In particular, the way religion organizes itself deserves our attention.

"I think I'm old enough to make my ***own*** decisions about going to church."

In the Old World, citizenship and church membership were products of the same simple process: being born. The church and the state existed in an uneasy alliance, dating all the way back to Constantine in the fourth century. Though who got to call the shots—the King or the Pope—occupied much of the contentious political discourse from the Middle Ages through the Protestant Reformation and beyond, it was always understood that some implicit relationship existed. The nature of that relationship was a matter of intense "negotiation" for a thousand years.

King: God chose me to administer God's justice—divine right and all that. Therefore, I'm in charge.

Pope: You're not the boss of me. God chose my office to administer God's wisdom—the head of Christ on earth and stuff. Therefore, I think you'll see, *I'm* in charge.

A new wrinkle, brought on by the intellectual battles of the Enlightenment, is the extent to which people are liberated not only from the European monarchy, but also from the (largely European) monarchical pretensions of the Church. Nowhere does this idea of religious freedom take root as strongly as in the New World. The idea of a state-sponsored church, a church in which baptism and citizenship mean roughly the same thing, comes under serious scrutiny in the colonies.

The impression that a cozy relationship between the monarchy and ecclesiastical hierarchy benefits only those in power gained purchase among virtually all religious groups, save the representatives of the Church of England. Presbyterians, Congregationalists, Baptists, Methodists, and eventually Lutherans begin to see that drawing the lines of religious freedom over a wider area profits everyone.[2] People begin to internalize this feeling of freedom, even going so far as to begin to suggest that freedom of religion also means freedom *from* religion.

---

[2]The historic Peace Churches, because of their pacifist commitments, tried to stay neutral but often found themselves pressured to take sides.

Thomas Jefferson famously enshrined this increasingly common sentiment in his Virginia Bill for Establishing Religious Freedom: "No man shall be compelled to frequent or support any religious worship, place, or ministry whatsoever, nor shall be inforced [sic], restrained, molested, or burthened in his body or goods, nor shall otherwise suffer of his religious opinions or belief" (Handy, 1977, 144). Notwithstanding the archaic language, it's easy to see that Thomas Jefferson opened the door to generations of Sunday golfers and *New York Times* readers. If nobody's making you go to church, if nobody's telling you that you're a Christian in virtue of being born in a nominally Christian country, if figuring out what and whom to believe occupies a new place in everyone's developmental model, the church is going to have to learn to do business differently.

All this emphasis on freedom is a mixed blessing for the church. On the one hand, whether intentionally or not, freedom prompts questions about the way religion has been traditionally organized as a power structure that continues to benefit those at the top. On the other hand, it also energizes people to begin to explore their faith as a pursuit for which they are now largely responsible, rather than as the passive recipients of a tradition they've had no hand in forming.

But before we examine the positive impact of all this newfound freedom on the church in America, we need to spend a little more time investigating the toll it took on the established church. Nowhere is the impact of the new suspicion of authority in the Revolutionary War more evident than the shifting attitudes toward clergy. For, as Thomas Jefferson pointed out, "Jesus was perfect for the republican era because he internalized morality. The law lay within the pure soul of each good citizen, not in the top-down commands of self-appointed clerics" (Fox, 2002, 65).

The Problem with Clergy

In the same way that the idea of royalty fell on hard times as a result of the American Revolution, the church's episcopal "royalty" (i.e., bishops, and by extension, their representatives, the parish clergy) also experienced a general decline in authority. The church hierarchy, rightly or wrongly, came to be associated with the tyranny many felt characterized rule by monarchy.

First, and most obviously, because the Church of England enjoyed state sponsorship, people opposed to the state easily transferred their ire for the king to the church.

"If the king pays your salary, the king owns you. And if the king owns you, you're part of the problem—not the solution."

Clergy from the Church of England were sent to the New World as missionaries. The clergy were, therefore, often much more conservative than their parishioners (Ahlstrom, 2004, 364)—conservative in the sense of invested in traditional church structures and church alliances with England. As a result, in the mind of the colonials, the clergy became proxies for the monarchy, eliciting some of the same contempt that people had stored up for the king. In fact, Robert Handy argues that the drive to appoint bishops was one of the causes, and not the effect, of dissatisfaction with England. He writes, "It was feared that if bishops came to the colonies they would snatch away liberties and reverse gains that had been made by other churches" (Handy, 1977, 136).

Second, though, and perhaps on a more abstract level, a general questioning of authority was bound to show up in a particular way in the church. The church, even without its ties to the imperial throne, had called the shots for over a thousand years by the time anybody from the Old World even knew there *was* such a thing as a New World. The church, as I mentioned earlier, had generated resentment among many because of its heavy-handedness on theological and political matters, as well as because of its intransigence on scientific matters.

The Enlightenment functioned for many as a nose-thumbing of epic proportions at the church—both Catholic and Protestant. In the New World, where many people came to escape their lives or to discover new lives in another place—lives that often had been lived under the thumb of one ecclesiastical or political authority or another—the idea of ceding control once again to authorities in a *new* place seemed unthinkable.

The clergy, as representatives of the very authority many immigrants were trying to leave behind, found the New World much less hospitable than the one they left. Country club memberships, for instance, were no longer automatic. (Besides, the golf courses were nothing more than cow pastures anyway.) The playing field in general no longer tilted quite so affirmatively in favor of the men of the cloth.

After the Revolutionary War, new Christian movements that had much less settled visions of ministry began to take root. Whereas the colonial mainline denominations—Congregationalists, Episcopalians, and Presbyterians—saw ministry as a vocation to be staffed by well-educated professionals who were seminary trained in the established schools that would eventually come to be known as the "Ivy League," the up-and-coming frontier denominations—Baptists, Methodists, and Disciples—tended to emphasize ministry as a calling to be pursued, the training for which would come along the way and largely at the hands of God, not some "fancy school back East." The practical effect of this difference on ministerial education was enormous. Because there were always more congregations than clergy, trained clergy among the colonial mainline were much in demand and could, therefore, afford to be choosy. They tended to go to well-established churches that paid the highest salaries, which more often than not were in the Northeast. Consequently, the culture of the colonial mainline churches inclined toward either stability or stagnation—depending on your perspective.

The frontier denominations, on the other hand, raised up ministers with an eye toward local contexts. These frontier ministers were rarely theologically trained in a formal setting, and they expected that ministry was inherently itinerant. As a result, frontier ministers were much more flexible in meeting the demands of whatever context they confronted. They had generally lower expectations about what the vocation of ministry could provide than their professional mainline colleagues (Finke and Stark, 2005, 84).

One especially difficult obstacle clergy in the Revolutionary War period faced was the growing popularity of Deism.

Deism: The Wonderful World of Cosmological Watchmaking

"Question with boldness even the existence of God," [Thomas Jefferson] urged his nephew in 1787, "because if there be one, he must more approve the homage of reason than that of blindfolded fear." (Carlson, 2011, 28)

Deism, as most people will vaguely recall from their eighth grade U.S. history course, was the attempt to marry reason and religion. The classic metaphor used to describe deism is the Watchmaker. It goes something like this: If you look at the world with anything like a discerning eye, you will quickly notice elegant patterns begin to emerge—the complexity of the body, or of the weather, or of the animal kingdom. It would be irrational to observe this complex elegance and fail to conclude that some intelligent being was behind its creation. On the other hand, it would be equally irrational to believe that this intelligent being was pulling levers all day long, manipulating the world supernaturally. Why? Because if the watchmaker were still causing all the gears to turn as they do, presumably the watchmaker could do a better job of making the gears mesh when it came to things like natural disasters and the DMV.

Isaac Newton, for instance, had proven that there were laws that operate in the universe that keep things stable and predictable. These laws don't depend on a supernatural being to make them work (they work just fine, thank you very much). Instead, deism said, the universe is like a watch, obviously made by a skilled watchmaker. After crafting the watch, however, the watchmaker wound it up and left it to run. The watch doesn't require the watchmaker to continually move the hands of the watch; it was made in such a way as to accomplish this task on its own—by design.

That is to say, according to the deists—who were flush with new knowledge of the natural world provided by people like Newton, and filled with the heady possibilities of reason and its application to public life that shows up in philosophers like John Locke—God need not be discarded altogether (Ahlstrom, 2004, 366). God is still theoretically possible, just not practically necessary anymore. In other words, people embarrassed by the long history of the church's superstitious and ham-fisted meddling in natural science found appealing the idea that it was no longer necessary to worry about God lurking around every corner.

"But that just sounds like a fancy way of being atheist."

I understand. But deism wasn't atheism; it was an attempt to satisfy the rigorous demands of reason without entirely abandoning faith.[3] It seemed like the best of both worlds, and consequently enjoyed some popularity among those who exercised leadership in America.

Wrightman Fox, writing about Thomas Jefferson—perhaps the most famous deist—argues that deism wasn't a capitulation to atheism, but an attempt to appropriate the teachings of Jesus in ways not ordinarily found in the church of the day. Jefferson, for instance, seemed to have a problem with the apparatus of religion, including such things as doctrine and clergy. He cared about Jesus, and what Jesus taught and did—not about the metaphysical speculation that had preoccupied so much of the church's life. In an environment suspicious of thoroughgoing atheism, Wrightman Fox contends:

---

[3]See Christopher Grasso's interesting article, "Deist Monster: On Religious Common Sense in the Wake of the American Revolution," *The Journal of American History* (June 2008), 43-68. In it Grasso explores the sensational story of late eighteenth century Deist, William Beadle, who killed his wife and four daughters before turning the gun on himself. He was held up as an example of the potential moral decay caused by deism. However, as Grasso points out, Beadle was anything but an atheist, believing that the murder of his children was simply turning them over to the care of God (59).

[Jesus] was a currency one could spend, a type of credit one could store up. Jefferson and Emerson wanted to show that a social critic should stand against certain religious structures and habits of mind without falling into French-style atheism. Appealing to Jesus gave legitimacy to their anticlerical liberalism. Of course the Gospel writers had made it easy for secularizers to sidle up to Jesus by depicting him as a rebel against conservative religious authority. Those like Jefferson and Emerson who wished to dissociate themselves from orthodox conceptions of divinity could proclaim, in effect, "Jesus made me do it." (Wrightman Fox, 2002, 63)

Anti-institutionalism. Ant-clericalism. An emphasis on Enlightenment reason. These hallmarks of deism also found expression, ironically, in the religious movements involved in the Second Great Awakening, albeit for different reasons. I will now turn to two of the founding documents of one of those movements, the Christian Church (Disciples of Christ).

2

Stone-Campbell and the Seeds of Reform

The period following the Revolutionary War saw the rise of the anti-establishment church in the newly founded United States of America. One of the characteristics of this new brand of church wasn't only its aversion to structure, but its belief that structure should serve mission; that if it should err, it should err on the side of generosity and freedom.

Baptists labored under the preacher-farmer model, which sought to minister on the frontier to whatever community the preacher happened to inhabit. Methodists used the "circuit rider" as a means of spreading the gospel, which favored the intensely difficult work of traveling to every outpost to preach the gospel to whoever could be found. Taking the lead of Barton Stone and the Campbells, early Disciples formed loose associations, the primary purpose of which included coming together for cooperation in the work of sharing the gospel.

Part of the interesting genius behind these cooperative Disciples associations was that the cooperation wasn't merely intended to be a pooling of resources for mission, but that the *cooperation* itself was one of the major tools of mission. That is to say, early Disciples believed that anything less than a united church hobbled the gospel—since who would take seriously religious expressions where the participants regularly fell out over, what onlookers often perceived to be, subtle points of doctrine.

Two documents helped lay the groundwork for the denomination that came to be known as the Christian Church (Disciples of Christ): *The Last Will and Testament of the Springfield Presbytery* and *The Declaration and Address.* These two documents focus on the issues of anti-institutionalism, anti-clericalism, and commonsense reason, as well as the unity of the church in ways that help to illustrate the kind of religious sensibilities present in the fertile ground from which springs the Second Great Awakening. This chapter briefly rehearses the original concerns expressed by these documents that gave rise to what eventually became the Disciples of Christ.

In this chapter, I describe how the churches led by Stone and Campbell arose as a reaction against the theological and ecclesiological commitments of the established institutional church. This reaction helped fuel—and was, in turn, fueled by—the religious phenomenon at the dawn of the nineteenth century called the Second Great Awakening. I use this chapter as a way to set the foundation upon which I will argue in chapter 3 that similar kinds of impulses that drove the revival of Christianity on the American frontier are impulses common to emerging generations.

Barton Stone and the Sunshine of the Presbyterianless Mind

Barton Warren Stone, a Maryland-born Presbyterian minister, tapped into the anti-institutionalism of the post-Revolutionary War period. As I pointed out in chapter 1, whether a casualty of the War for Independence or a cause of it, Americans bridled under received traditions and hierarchical authority. And nowhere was received tradition and hierarchical authority more apparent than in the institutional Protestantism that had quickly become part of the cultural backbone of the early colonies.

Though religious freedom had long been a rallying cry of the American colonists, its pursuit had largely been individual expressions of self-preservation. That is to say, originally the *idea* of religious freedom had less to do with giving all people access to the religion of their choosing than with allowing individual Protestant denominations a place to carve out their own institutional hegemonies (i.e., "A place where we finally get to be the boss"). Three Protestant denominations in particular experienced success in establishing institutional beachheads in the New World: Anglicans, Congregationalists, and Presbyterians.

These Protestant denominations, for instance, weren't opposed to state sponsorship. They liked the financial backing of the government as much as any European religious monolith. They just wanted their own territories to control, which because of history and the lack of space, their European homelands had largely denied them. Consequently, from the start these new champions of religious freedom were almost always more concerned with securing their own freedom than with extending it to others.

"Well, we're here. Long journey. But we're ready to build our church. Where should we go to set up?"

"What kind of church do you intend to set up?"

"Mennonite?"

"Oh, I'm sorry. This is a Congregationalist state. If you want to be Mennonite, you're going to have to go to...Let's see. Oh, that's right. There aren't any Mennonite states. If you're interested in becoming Congregationalist, though, we could set you up."

Over time, however, the political problems with authority and received tradition became *religious* problems. The established churches of the colonies suffered a loss of members and influence as Enlightenment ideals took hold and as people moved away from the power centers in the East to the spacious territories of the West.

The Christian Church (Disciples of Christ) emerged at the turn of the nineteenth century as an indigenous, and thoroughly American, religious movement. Perhaps the symbolic birth of the movement happened in 1804 when Barton Stone dropped "Presbyterian minister" from his résumé and became simply "Christian minister," simultaneously capturing the anti-authoritarian, anti-institutional spirit of the age.

Stone—though he came to understand the necessity of salvation from the fires of Hell through the fervent preaching of the Presbyterian, James McGready—found one of the central tenets of Calvinist Presbyterianism of the time problematic: namely, that salvation is entirely a result of God's initiative, leaving no room for the individual to choose God. He was persuaded of his need for God. Nevertheless, Stone struggled with this theological hurdle as it eroded his confidence that he could pursue salvation, since God had to make the first move—the-gospel-as-always-potentially-lousy-news.

Eventually, however, Stone had something of an epiphany when he heard William Hodge preach about the love of God—not an entirely novel practice. However, what resonated with Stone was the absence of an emphasis on the negative consequences associated with a particularly detailed description of Hell—a standard homiletical set-piece at the time. As McAllister and Tucker suggest, "It became clear to him that the Gospel really was good news, good news for him. He was converted" (McAllister and Tucker, 1975, 64).

Having entered school to become a lawyer, Stone ultimately sought and received ordination in the Presbyterian Church. His influences tended, not toward the rigidity he associated with confessional Protestantism, but toward toleration. Mark Toulouse writes that Stone's pastoral mentors

> reflected the prevailing American mind-set. They were liberal in their attitudes toward the doctrines of others, respecting the individual's right to search for and define a personal understanding of the religious truth. Though they were deeply concerned to communicate the gospel in clear unmistakable ways, they were not much interested in defending creedal orthodoxy. (Toulouse, 1997, 23-24).

Barton Stone's reticence about his Presbyterian ordination continued to mount, influenced by the Arminianism of the increasingly popular Methodist Church, which argued for both the individual's role in salvation as well as for a "simple and heartfelt faith" (Garrison and DeGroot, 1969, 96). Stone became convinced that the new energy associated with "camp meetings" (i.e., Revivalism) promised a way out of the lethargy Christianity had experienced on the frontier.

At the turn of the nineteenth century, religion still had yet to rebound from its nadir during the Revolutionary War and its aftermath. Kentucky, for instance, where Stone went as pastor of the churches at Cane Ridge and Concord, probably saw only 4 to 5 percent of its inhabitants claim church membership at the time (McAllister and Tucker, 1975, 69).

Seeking some way of spurring spiritual passion in his parishes, Barton Stone traveled to Logan County, Kentucky, to witness a revival. Having seen the energy and vitality of this revival, Stone returned home and soon hosted a revival at his own parish at Cane Ridge in August of 1801—an event McAllister and Tucker call the climax of the Second Great Awakening (71). The Cane Ridge revival drew between 20,000 and 30,000 people over the course of its five days. People gathered to hear preaching and to socialize. The emotional response to the event evoked great shows of passion (shouting, jerking, barking, laughing), with conversions estimated at "between one thousand and two thousand" (72). Pastors from a variety of denominations—Baptists, Presbyterians, Methodists—preached to enthusiastic crowds. Stone was greatly moved by the religious energy unleashed by the revival. And though he displayed ambivalence about the more emotional expressions of devotion, he was also impressed by the ability of different denominations to work and worship together, focusing not on their theological differences, but being drawn together by their commitment to God (Toulouse, 1997, 26).

However, this denominational intermingling—in particular the practice of allowing the uncredentialed (i.e, unordained men who had never produced proof of either education or theological orthodoxy) to preach—caught the attention of disapproving Presbyterians. Many Presbyterians saw the looseness as a potential threat to orthodoxy. A preacher, who would ordinarily have to undergo a thorough vetting at the hands of a panel of ordained clerics, could come to a revival, without benefit of official sanction, and start preaching. In other words, the criterion of readiness to preach at a revival had clearly shifted, from a focus on the proper educational and ecclesiastical pedigree to a focus on the preacher's ability to persuade.

"Before you ascend the sacred desk, we need to see your membership card and the secret handshake."

"Huh?

"Your seminary transcripts and your ordination credentials."

"I didn't go to seminary; although I did complete a blacksmith correspondence course. Plus, I got my ordination certificate from a guy who was selling re-purposed wristwatches."

"You can't preach, then."

"Why not? I've got something to say."

*"We'll decide whether you have something to say. In fact, we'll tell you **when** you've got something to say, and with just how much enthusiasm we require of you to say it."*

Stone saw this willingness to accept preachers from other traditions—even traditions with vastly different understandings of ordination—as a positive thing. In the midst of preaching the gospel, denominational boundary maintenance ceased to be an issue. Opening up the pulpit to non-sanctioned preachers shifted the focus off of parochial differences and onto the unifying nature of the gospel.

In 1804, for example, after Stone and the other Presbyterian ministers broke away from the General Assembly of Presbyterians, the Assembly sent a committee seeking to reconcile with the representative ministers of the disbanded Springfield Presbytery. The committee asked some questions. The second question and the answer to it suggests just how different Stone's vision of unity was from the one held by the established church:

> Question 2. By the committee of the general Assembly. "Can any method of accommodation be proposed, which may induce you to return to the jurisdiction of that church, and heal the division which has taken place in the Synod of Kentucky?"

What follows is part of the answer to that question. It argues that the action taken to disassociate from the Synod, far from being divisive, actually opened up the range of their inclusion beyond "party" (i.e., denominational) lines to include all Christians.

> We feel ourselves citizens of the world, God our common Father, all men our brethren by nature, and all christians our brethren in Christ. This principle of universal love to christians, gains ground in our hearts in proportion as we get clear of particular attachments to a party. (Stone and Rogers, 1847, 41)

Among the other complaints lodged against revivalism was the charge that it misled people into thinking that they had any amount of control over their ability to come to God. According to Calvinist orthodoxy, God took responsibility for salvation—without the need for human input. Revivalism, on the other hand, stressed the individual's ability to seek out God for salvation, "that 'Christ died for all,' contrary to the orthodox Calvinistic teaching that only a limited number, the elect, were the objects of redeeming grace" (Garrison and DeGroot, 1969, 102).

"Can we help you?"

"I heard about this Jesus character, and I think I'd like to know a bit more. He sounds like my kind of guy."

"The thing is … Jesus is kind of particular about who he keeps company with. We can't let you into the party without an invitation. You're not on our list. Sorry. There's a prison down the street. If you go there, I'm pretty sure they'll have your name on the list."

Barton Warren Stone, born on Christmas Eve, 1772, was truly a child of the Revolution. Temperamentally, he resisted heavy-handed hierarchy, trusting in the sensibilities of ordinary folks both to know and to choose their religious paths. This democratizing impulse was nowhere more evident for Stone than in his handling of the controversy with the Presbyterian

Synod of Kentucky and the subsequent founding (and dissolution) of the Springfield Presbytery.

In the aftermath of the controversy over revivalism, Richard McNemar and John Thompson, two of Stone's Presbyterian clergy colleagues, walked out of a Kentucky Synod meeting in which they were central subjects in a debate over the heretical nature of Revivalism. The resulting protest, signed by a total of five Presbyterian ministers (including Barton Stone), disassociated themselves from the Kentucky Synod "until, through the providence of God, it seem good to your reverend body to adopt a more liberal plan, respecting human Creeds and Confessions" (McAllister and Tucker, 1975,75).

In the fall of 1803, the five dissenters formed their own ecclesiastical body, the Springfield Presbytery, which, within ten months and after adding another minister to the cause, they just as quickly disbanded. By the time they dissolved the Springfield Presbytery, however, these ministers and their churches had ceased to be Presbyterians and claimed only to be "Christians." I will say more about what I take to be the implications of the disbanding of the Springfield Presbytery for a post-denominational world in chapter 4. However, here I want to explore some of the interesting reasons the six ministers gave for "breaking up the band." That the Springfield Presbytery ceased to exist after ten months isn't particularly noteworthy; religious organizations form and then later disband all the time. But the reason for this swift separation, as well as the manner by which it was achieved, deserves analysis.

Only a short time after detaching themselves from the Presbyterian Synod of Kentucky, the ministers of the newly formed Springfield Presbytery arrived at the conclusion that though they had separated themselves from hierarchical denominational authority, they had only succeeded in setting up a potentially new system of hierarchical authority. That they considered themselves to be good guys only meant that the new hierarchy differed in degree rather than in kind from the very structure they deplored. In other words, six ministers, under no external pressure to do so, came to the conclusion that if they continued as a Presbytery, they would be (either in principle or, eventually, in practice) no better than the people they sought to distance themselves from—a refreshing, if rare, moment of ecclesiastical self-awareness.

Here is the opening claim of the document, which then proceeds to set down reasons for the dissolution: "We will, that this body die, be dissolved, and sink into union with the Body of Christ at large; for there is but one body, and one Spirit, even as we are called in one hope of our calling."

Just as importantly as the dissolution of the Springfield Presbytery, however, were the issues they found important enough to name as fundamental to church organization. From a theological standpoint, *The Last Will and Testament* identified the Bible as the measure of faithful life and doctrine. As far as they were concerned, creeds (they would say "human creeds") would no longer rival Scripture as the final bar of authority for life and faith. If you wanted to know what God thought about how you should live or how the church should organize itself, all you needed to do was go to the Bible and check. Otherwise, you risked letting "human innovations" slip in through the back door.[1]

But chief among the ideas prized by the "Springfield Six," and especially important for my purposes, was the privileging of freedom and the severing of authority for congregational life from larger denominational structures. Like the politics that inspired rebellion against the tyranny of monarchy in the Revolutionary War, the Second Great Awakening experienced a rebellion against the tyranny of ecclesiastical hierarchy. Stone and his compatriots were socialized in a new world that prized the freedom of the individual to make choices. As I've noted, the expanded horizons introduced by the Enlightenment and the United States' willingness to stand up to its British cousins opened up not only political horizons but religious ones as well. The idea that individuals—and by extension, congregations—had not only the opportunity, but the *right* to have a free hand in choosing a destiny for themselves, increasingly seemed to many to be the way God had ordered the universe. And even a casual reading of the Bible appeared to affirm this conviction (see, for example, Joshua 24:15).

In a nutshell, then, *The Last Will and Testament of the Springfield Presbytery* set down a vision of the church that looked to the Bible and not to human creeds or denominational customs to order its life. This reliance upon the Bible also buttressed a freedom not only *from* the infrastructure of denominations but also a freedom *to* reimagine the purpose and ministry of the church. Instead of expending time, energy, and money propping up what they felt to be an arbitrary and unjust denominational system, they were able to focus their attention on the mission of the Gospel.

---

[1] It's worth pointing out that this Enlightenment view of our ability to understand texts in a common sense way, though we now realize was overly optimistic about our abilities to shed our own presuppositions on command, was a reaction to centuries of tradition about who could interpret the Bible. The Enlightenment extended the belief put forward in the Reformation that ordinary people could be trusted to understand Scripture without the ecclesiastical training wheels provided by the church and its multilayered interpretive apparatus.

In chapter 4 I want to look further at some of the similarities between the impulse that led to the dissolution of the Springfield Presbytery and what mainline denominations can anticipate in a post-denominational world. Without advocating for the collapse of denominations, I will point out a potentially positive outcome from the continued weakening of denominational ties: Fewer resources consumed by denominational infrastructures might mean the unleashing of an enormous amount of religious and financial energy, which could then be focused directly on mission.

Thomas Campbell: Your Table Is Ready

Thomas and Alexander Campbell, from County Down, Ireland, came to the new world after the turn of the nineteenth century. Thomas arrived first in Pennsylvania and was later followed by his son, Alexander.

Thomas quickly received an appointment to preach in Washington County, Pennsylvania, and soon found himself embroiled in controversy after admitting to communion Presbyterians of varying stripes.

"I'd like to partake of the Lord's Supper."

"Presbyterian affiliation?"

"New Light Burgher Non-seceder."

"The body of our Lord broken for you . . ."

"That's it?"

"Well, there's the cup too."

"Are you sure you can give this to me?"

"We're out in the middle of nowhere. What are they going to do, fire me?"

In March 1808, Thomas Campbell was effectively fired, or at least suspended, pending an investigation. That Thomas proved scandalously undiscerning in the stewardship of the table to the Presbyterian way of thinking caused a committee of the Chartiers Presbytery to bring charges of heresy against him.

Campbell argued at an Associate Synod in May that the authority by which ecclesiastical decisions ought to be made derived entirely from Scripture. In fact, he contended that if the church were to be united, it would be solely on the basis of Scripture and not on the basis of creeds and confessions created by human beings (implied: like the weasels who were jamming him up over communion).

In September 1808, the Associate Synod permanently suspended Thomas Campbell. As McAllister and Tucker and note, though, "Campbell's withdrawal from the presbytery and synod, however, brought no interruption in his ministerial labors" (McAllister and Tucker, 1975, 110). In that simple sentence, McAllister and Tucker capture the heart of the religious movement that emerged from the religious vortex of doom following the Revolutionary War. That Thomas Campbell didn't blink when dismissed from the Presbyterian structure responsible for authorizing clergy credentials and appointments is worthy of comment.

What do I mean by that?

I find it interesting that Thomas Campbell, as well as Barton Stone before him, valued their attachments to the Presbyterian denominational structure. Being authorized as ministers of the Gospel was something Stone and Campbell sought out and took seriously once they obtained it. They certainly expended an enormous amount of energy attempting to convince the power behind the religious structure that they were orthodox. In short, Stone and Campbell wanted to remain Presbyterians . . . until it became clear to them that to do so would require selling out their principles.

Rather than forswear their hard won theological insights, Stone and Campbell abandoned denominationalism. They determined that they had more to gain from being unassociated than from conforming themselves at all cost, just so they could keep their appointments. They preferred to walk away from a structure that no longer served true ministry, but persisted in its preoccupation with an orthodoxy that appeared to have less and less to do with helping the world hear about Jesus—an impulse to which contemporary emerging generations have continued to respond.

After leaving the Presbyterians, Thomas Campbell wrote over the following year a document entitled *The Declaration and Address*, which was to stand as a foundational document for the newly formed and self-consciously non-denominational *Christian Association of Washington*. The Christian Association, founded by Thomas Campbell, sought to bring Christians together in a loose confederation, not in order to impose another layer of ecclesiastical bureaucracy on congregations, but to provide some formal ties by which they could aid and assist one another in ministry. *The Declaration and Address* lays down some principles that would guide this new Christian Association:

1. The right of private judgment

2. The sole authority of Scripture

3. The evil of sectarianism

4. The basis for Christian unity in exact conformity to the Bible[2]

Notice how these themes arise in the above list:

1. The freedom of the individual, over against the church

2. The basis for speaking authoritatively about what it means to think and live like a Christian comes directly from a common sense reading of the Bible rather than from some human innovation—no matter how well conceived—set down as church orthodoxy

3. The assumption that division in the church is bad, not just because it causes dissension and distrust, but because that dissension and distrust belie the very integrity of the body of Christ

4. The foundation upon which unity exists resides, not in the ability of Christians to develop newer and more sophisticated theologies, but upon their simple belief that the Bible offers the only real standard around which to rally

Again, I want to draw attention to the underlying philosophical assumptions: (1) faith is found in the individual's pursuit of God, and not through the elaborate organization of a "human system," and (2) the church fails to live up to its vocation when it seeks unanimity rather than unity. These two concerns—association with a community of believers rather than denominational membership, and unity rather than doctrinal purity—remain extremely important to emerging generations today.

In the next chapter I'll take a look at some of the connections between the cultural and religious climate of the post-Revolutionary War era and the post-denominational world in which we find ourselves today.

---

[2]I am relying here on the summary of *The Declaration and Address* given in McAllister and Tucker, 112.

3

What Can We Learn?

Taming the Chihuahua Brain

As I sat at the kitchen table yesterday reading the newspaper, I heard one of our dogs barking outside on the deck. We have five dogs, so hearing a dog barking just outside the kitchen isn't particularly noteworthy. Our dogs are so sensitive that they bark at cross-eyed gnats. Their behavior annoys the neighbors.

I got up to let the dog in so he'd stop ruining everyone's leisurely Saturday morning. As I opened the door, I noticed a man I didn't recognize walking away from our neighbor's garage. I found our six-pound Chihuahua delivering, what I'm sure he intended to be, a bracing message of warning. The strange man looked back over his shoulder at me and hurried down the driveway. Something didn't feel quite right about the stranger's presence.

As I walked back into my house, I remember observing, "Well, maybe the dogs get it right once in awhile." I don't suppose I'll ever know.

The whole thing got me thinking, though. Evolution has honed canine senses to acute levels.[1] They are so sensitive, in fact, that they respond to any new stimulus as a threat—and they can sniff out a threat a mile away. Living in the wild, constant vigilance against natural enemies is evolutionarily advantageous. Living in a suburban home, on the other hand, where the

---

[1]It has been called the "lizard brain" or the "triune brain," but I have more experience observing Chihuahuas, so I'll stick with "Chihuahua brain" for the purposes of this text/ (http://www.buffalostate.edu/orgs/bcp/brainbasics/triune.html).

fiercest threat is the neighbor's dachshund three yards over, constant vigilance is maladaptive behavior. Besides, what exactly could a six-pound Chihuahua save me from anyway?

Noting the highly sensitive threat detection systems that patrol our backyard, people have said, "You've got some good watchdogs." Usually I smile and nod my head. What I want to say, however, is: "No, they're not. They're horrible watchdogs. If everything makes them bark, then they're useless as watchdogs." Fear only works as an effective warning signal if there's truly something to be afraid of. To walk around in a perpetual state of fear is exhausting, and sustained long-term stress is damaging to the body; it releases all sorts of chemicals that are helpful for short-term confrontations with genuine threats. But perpetual stress is corrosive (http://psychcentral. com/lib/2007/the-physical-effects-of-long-term-stress/). Prolonged stress has been linked to heart disease, hypertension, stroke, cancer, diabetes, gastrointestinal disorders, as well as sexual dysfunction (http://www.umm. edu/patiented/articles/what_health_consequences_of_stress_000031_3. html). In other words, thinking that everything will kill you will eventually kill you. In addition to the physical impairments caused by prolonged stress, the psychological toll can be debilitating. If you're afraid all the time, you lose perspective about what to be afraid of and when it's appropriate. It's possible, in other words, to be afraid of, and react with hostility to, things that are good for you—and inevitably to tune out real threats.

Pattern Recognition, the Herd, and the Threat of Change

Michael Shermer, a famous skeptic and psychologist, has popularized the insight surrounding pattern recognition. Humans, he suggests, are pattern-recognition machines. With any set of inputs—sight, sound, taste, touch, smell—the human brain is set to identify patterns. Amidst the noise and chaos of everyday life, humans are amazingly adept at picking out patterns. That's why parents in a crowded McDonalds can distinguish the scream of their child amid the screams of a herd of other children. It's why when you're driving faster than you're supposed to and you look in the rearview mirror and see the distinctive grille of a Crown Victoria in the rearview mirror, you automatically take your foot off the gas pedal. Babies, for example, at one day old will focus on edges and stripes (http://www.psychologytoday.com/ blog/imagine/201103/what-s-the-pattern). Within a relatively short period of time, they are able to distinguish the faces and voices of their parents from other faces and voices in an already crowded world.

From an evolutionary standpoint, pattern recognition is essential to survival. If you're stumbling about in the African Savannah and you hear something in the bush, you have a choice to make.

1. You can assume it's a predator, and take appropriate action.

2. You can assume it's the wind, and ignore it.

Shermer says that if you choose to believe it's a predator but it turns out to be the wind, you haven't really lost much except a little extra adrenaline. On the other hand, if you choose to believe it's the wind and it turns out to be a tiger … well, your genes have to get out of the pool.

Consequently, humans have developed a keen ability to find patterns everywhere since the cost of being wrong about danger is too high. Unfortunately, while this kind of super-tuned threat detection is helpful for survival in an environment where the chances of being eaten are genuinely great, it doesn't serve us nearly so well when the biggest threats we face day to day aren't *real* aggression but passive aggression—when the threat isn't that we'll be eaten but that the yogurt we left in the fridge for our afternoon break will be eaten by Janice, who apparently finds it impossible to leave her hands off other people's stuff. (Thought: Perhaps leaving a sarcastic sign on the fridge about eating only your own food might ….) In modern life we're much more prone to pattern recognition that ensures not our safety but our comfort level. I take it that that's why most of us are so ill-disposed to change. Change represents a break in the pattern, and therefore a potential threat—if not to my safety, then to my sense that the world is a hospitable place and basically designed to provide me a disruption-free existence.

It occurs to me that the church—denominational and congregational—especially those parts of the church experiencing decline, tend to confront the world with the nervous system of a six-pound Chihuahua, treating each new change in the environment as a threat. They've evolved highly sensitive threat detectors over time. Unfortunately, these threat detectors issue an unacceptable level of false-positives.

If you bought a pregnancy test, for instance, that gave you a false-positive 90% of the time, you'd quit using it. If you had a security system that went off every time the baby cried or the parakeet belched, you'd be on the phone imploring your provider for an emergency service call to recalibrate the sensors. Threat detectors that go off indiscriminately and often are useless (at best), and crazy-making (at worst).

Why do churches settle, then, for a life wired to respond to every new thing like a six-pound dog, certain that calamity is behind every bush?

The only way to tame the Chihuahua brain is to relinquish control of the future to God. "For those who want to save their life will lose it, and those who lose their life for my sake will find it" (Matt. 16:25). In other words, thinking that everything will kill you ... will eventually kill you. It's God's church, after all. God's plenty capable of taking care of God's stuff. What exactly could I save God from anyway?

Mainline denominations in a perennial state of decline have cause for concern. Congregations that continue to lose members year after year have good reason for self-reflection. Unfortunately, though, the kind of slump I'm talking about often prompts not vigilant and thoughtful assessment, but indiscriminate panic. Every change gets identified as a potential threat.

But change, as we know, is exactly what's needed.

In this chapter I will explore the changes that took place in post-Revolutionary War America, changes that set the stage for the emergence of an invigorated Christianity. Then I will set those historical changes beside the sorts of changes taking place in the world we now inhabit. I will argue that those changes present an opportunity for declining mainline denominations and their congregations to embrace the inevitable changes rather than reflexively fear them.

What? More History?

The people in charge were scared. How could they avoid it? Many of the important assumptions about how the world operated had fallen on hard times. The Revolutionary War produced a number of casualties—and not all of them human. The conceptual landscape was also littered with the corpses of dead ideas and traditions.

In fact, the changes on the cultural and religious landscape were so profound that the language used to speak about them evoked images of the end times. Hatch argues that "it was not merely the winning of battles and the writing of constitutions that excited apocalyptic visions in the minds of ordinary people but the realization that the very structures of society were undergoing a democratic winnowing. Political convulsions seemed cataclysmic; the cement of an ordered society seemed to be dissolving" (Hatch, 1989, 6). In other words, the New World, in more ways than just geographically, really was a *new world*.

Gone, for instance, was the assumption that being born well conferred special status. As I've noted, before the Revolution, society was built on rigidly defined and observed class distinctions and deference to established centralized authority (crown and church). After the Revolution, however, the fact that your parents had a membership at the yacht club might buy you extra courtesy, to be sure. However, it didn't mean any longer that you were fundamentally superior to the guy mucking out stalls down at the local stables.

It bears repeating that this newfound affection for egalitarianism did not extend so far as to include women or non-white Protestant males. However, if you were white, male, and Protestant (preferably of English descent), you had a cocktail and a front row seat to the dawning of a new era in human history. And while the theoretical possibilities surrounding equality outpaced the practical realities—and in many ways still do—that the *idea* of equality became a conceptual possibility signaled a radical overhaul of the traditional assumptions about the nature of human beings. Democracy and its ideals prevailed. The politics and religion of the established order took a tremendous thrashing at the hands of those who warmed to the idea of egalitarianism. No longer could a man depend upon his station in life to gain a hearing.[2] Democracy, by its very nature, highlighted the emphasis on human equality. As I've mentioned in the previous chapters, the idea of hierarchical authority and the priority of tradition took a backseat to new populist ideas about "who gets to be the boss," and whether that authority comes from someplace other than "because that's the way we've always done it." The Revolution and its aftermath largely deconstructed the presumption of hierarchical authority.

This stress on egalitarianism found its way into the church. Nathan Hatch writes: "Christianity was effectively reshaped by common people who molded it in their own image and who threw themselves into expanding its influence. Increasingly assertive common people wanted their leaders unpretentious, their doctrines self-evident and down-to-earth, their music lively and singable, and their churches in local hands" (Hatch, 1989, 9).

However, aversion to hierarchical authority in the church didn't just affect organization. As long as Christians were doing a little house cleaning on the issue of leadership authority, they also called into question the authority of "human traditions" when it came to doctrine. You can't just dismiss the

---

[2] I use man advisedly here, since, again, using "women" and "leader" as correlatives in a sentence would have been conceptually impossible.

bosses without taking a look at the bosses' rules. Leadership authority and the authority of tradition were intimately linked.

After the Revolution, the creeds and confessions employed by established denominations, in many cases, had to find justification not just in longstanding traditions but in the Bible. As in the case of the Burgher/ Anti-burgher or the Seceder/Non-seceder controversies in Presbyterianism— articles of faith based on local political controversies rather than arguments over biblical doctrine—people began to question the legitimacy of non-biblical traditions as litmus tests for Christian faithfulness. In fact, so ingrained had the anti-establishment impulse become that many people were dubious of *any* orthodoxy that originated in the establishment.

Fruit from the poisonous tree. In the legal world this means that all inferences drawn from tainted evidence are themselves tainted. In this case, the thinking seemed to be that corrupt systems produce corrupt dogma. However, the "You-should-do-what-we-say-even-though-we've-always-treated-common-people-like-crap" line of thinking apparently had difficulty gaining traction in the New World.

Rebelling against received tradition went hand in hand with the inclination to expand geographic boundaries. Migration to the frontier, though clearly a decision to recalibrate the settled economics of the class system, also landed a symbolic blow against the political and religious establishment. Whatever the reason, whether because they wanted to put some distance between themselves and the ruling class by taking to the frontier, or because the practical effect of taking to the frontier was to put some distance between themselves and the ruling class, the settlers found themselves increasingly disconnected from the systems of power—political and religious—which just a few years before had been taken for granted as a part of everyone's lives.

Moving out into the vast expanses of the unexplored frontier demonstrated enormous imagination and courage. That people looked at the seemingly unending line of mountains in the Appalachian Mountain chain, then at their families packed into wagons, and said, "That doesn't look so bad. I think we can do this," bespeaks an enormous amount of creative thinking and a breathtaking belief in their capacity for endurance.

Stick It to the Man!

Ok. Enough history for a moment.

You may be wondering why I would take so long and plow through so much history surrounding the Revolutionary War and the Second Great

Awakening that followed. Simply put, I think there are striking similarities between that period of history at the start of the nineteenth century and the period in which we now live at the start of the twenty-first century.

As I've said, the time around the Revolutionary War and its aftermath saw the church in America at arguably its lowest point in history:

- The Enlightenment called into question the traditional claim that faith and revelation stood at the epistemological center. The church, which had to that point relied on its position of authority as the interpreter of revealed faith, suffered when reason emerged as the new epistemological center.

- Politics also took center stage culturally. The move from monarchy to democracy represented a seismic political shift. The implications of locating the authority to rule in the hands of the people, which wrested authority from the hands of traditional rulers—both political and religious—can hardly be overstated. The church declined as people turned their attention to a new form of social organization that didn't assume the necessity of religious input.

- The church lost a lot of its shine by being too closely aligned, not only with an unpopular political tradition, but more broadly with tradition itself. Culturally and politically, newly minted Americans lived in heady times. Everything felt altered and new. Horizons were boundless and full of possibility. Ideas were novel and compelling. How could the church, which had been around forever, compete?

This brief description of Christianity in post-Revolutionary War America, with a couple of strategically placed substitutions, would be a serviceable description of Christianity in contemporary America. Taking the temperature of mainline Christianity in America, for instance, it feels to many as though its best days lay in the past, especially among emerging generations.

The most recent *Pew Forum on Religion & Public Life* reveals that one in five Americans have no religious affiliation (http://www.pewforum.org/Unaffiliated/nones-on-the-rise.aspx). Among those under the age of thirty, the number rises to one in three. Over the past five years, "Unaffiliated" is the fastest growing segment of the population.[3]

---

[3]"Unaffiliated" includes atheists and agnostics (6%) and nothing in particular or the "Nones" (14%).

Some important statistics:

- Millennials are three times more likely to be "Unaffiliated" than their parents and grandparents over the age of 65, while Gen X-ers are twice as likely.

- White Protestants (Mainline and Evangelical) have reason to take notice of this decline not simply because fewer people are identifying as Christian but because over the past forty years the Unaffiliated have increased by 11% at the same time as white Protestants have declined by 9%.

- Moreover, white Protestants shouldn't take much comfort from the belief that marketing is at the root of the problem. That is to say, the idea that "What we've got is a good thing; we're just not packaging it correctly for younger people," since 88% of the Unaffiliated say they're not in the market for religion at all—marketed more snappily or otherwise.

Attitudes toward the church in the contemporary period track well with attitudes toward the church in the post-Revolutionary War period:

- Though the Enlightenment emphasis on reason has dominated epistemology in academia over the past two hundred years, and to a lesser extent in the culture, a significant portion of the population has continued to hold the traditional view that when faith and science clash, science must change. Unaffiliateds, who tend to be more socially and politically liberal, view the loss of religion's influence on society as a good thing by a two-to-one margin over the general public.

- Though seismic political shifts that preoccupy the culture's attention, like the one moving from monarchy to democracy, haven't taken place, there is something new on the cultural horizon that is preoccupying the culture's attention with the same kind of intensity—that is, culture itself. With the advent of the Internet and twenty-four-hour cable television programming (news, in particular), the culture is always encroaching. Reality TV. Politics. Sports. Home improvement. Cooking. The entertainment industry has sought to provide programming fit to scratch the itch of virtually any desire. In fact, in an amazingly "meta" way, the entertainment industry has turned itself into a ubiquitous opportunity for cultural consumption. With so many options vying for our attention, the church's plea to follow a first-century rabbi cannot but appear as overly simplistic and unentertaining to a culture preoccupied with itself, and even preoccupied by its own preoccupation with itself—the cultural version of the vortex of doom.

- Part of the problem faced by the church in contemporary times has not only to do with the amazing capacity of the culture to draw attention to itself—at least some of which attention in other eras would have been focused on the church—but with the fact that, since the cultural upheaval of the 1960s, the church has once again been negatively identified with the received tradition of the establishment. The decline of mainline Protestantism began as the message took hold that the established denominational church—as it did in the Revolutionary Era—had been complicit with the political establishment in attempting to retain its power and control at the expense of such natural Christian moral issues as civil rights, women's equality, our part in the ecological havoc wreaked on the environment by industry, and opposition to an unpopular war. If the church were only the religious arm of the political and cultural establishment, as many supposed, unable to raise its voice in opposition to evils it appeared to have every reason to oppose, many began to wonder why thoughtful people ought to have anything to do with it. The church's silence on these issues prompted people to begin questioning not only the relevance of the church and its moral authority, but whether it had outlived its usefulness. On the other hand, to be fair, it should be noted that there were individuals within the established mainline denominational church as it began experiencing decline who opposed what they viewed as the acculturation of the church. In the 1960s movements within the mainline churches spoke out prophetically against the church's silence and inaction on issues of racism, feminism, environmentalism, and opposition to the war.

- Other contemporary criticisms align with the criticisms of the church at the turn of the nineteenth century. Currently, the popular cultural stance of suspicion toward authority finds similarities in the attitudes in post-Revolutionary War America toward the British monarchy and its colonial proxies. As the pioneers moved westward on the frontier, they put distance between themselves and ecclesiastical authority. When the clergy from the colonial establishment later showed up, the pioneers—who had done "just fine, thank you very much" without clerical or denominational oversight—failed to assume the traditional deference to the church.

"We need you to help build our new church in town."

"I have neither the time nor the inclination to build you a church."

"But the church needs you. As a Christian, you are expected to support the church."

"I traveled for the better part of a year, through mountain passes in the winter, and swampy bogs in the spring. I had to fight my way through dense forests and ford swollen streams, and sleep in the snow. I lost two children and five animals along the way. I built this house and cleared this land with only my family and these two hands. And here's the thing: nobody got to tell me how to do any of it. I did it myself. And I aim to continue to live that way. So, as a man without a gun, you are expected to get the hell off my property."

Contemporary Americans are rarely called upon to defer to ecclesiastical authority, nor would they likely consider it any more than their early American ancestors did. One of the defining features of the Revolutionary Era was a reorientation of the cultural attitudes toward authority, from one of unquestioning submission to authority to one of skeptical resistance to authority.

Suspicion of authority persisted as a part of the American psyche through much of the 1800s and the expansion of the frontier. However, the Industrial Revolution—with the automation and mass production of the factories, with the rise of specialization and assembly lines, with the advent of foremen and time clocks—saw a return to a footing in which capitulation to authority was once again assumed.

Since the 1960s, though, a return to skepticism of authority has emerged. From the Postmodernism of Jacques Derrida and Jean-François Lyotard to the Post-Structuralism of Michel Foucault, suspicion of authority and received tradition made a big comeback. This revolution in ideas played out in popular culture in the form of slogans offered as appeals to question authority:

- "Power to the People!"

- "Hell no, we won't go!" (in response to the Vietnam War)

- "Do your own thing."

- "Stick it to the man!"

In speaking about Steve Jobs, U2 singer Bono gives an apt description of the impact of the anti-authoritarianism of the 1960s on American culture:

> The people who invented the twenty-first century were pot-smoking, sandal-wearing hippies from the West Coast like Steve, because they saw differently," he said. "The hierarchical systems of the East Coast, England, Germany, and Japan do not encourage this different thinking. The sixties produced an anarchic mind-set that is great for imagining a world not yet in existence. (Isaacson, 65)

But contemporary resistance to clergy and any unwillingness to submit to them—when it doesn't originate in some scandal or hypocrisy—generally has less to do with strong anti-clerical feelings than with the belief that the church and its emissaries are largely irrelevant. In the past, people opposed the clergy as a symbol of the authority of the monarchy. At present, people ignore clergy as a symbol of the authority of a tradition that no longer matters much. The question of hierarchical authority in America has long been settled in favor of anti-authoritarianism to such an extent that it is almost transparent to us anymore. We just assume it. So, while modern American culture no longer defers to clergy, it has less to do with the idea of clergy as symbols of institutional power than with the fact that, for many, clergy remain as remnants of a bygone world—a world in which revelation and faith trump reason.

As I've mentioned, the move to settle the frontier offered distance from institutionalized authority. And while heading west offered the pioneers freedom *from* the kind of hierarchical power that just a few years earlier had been taken for granted, it also represented to them freedom *for* something. The frontier promised a chance to create something of one's own. Because of the static nature of the class system, advancement had traditionally come not because of ingenuity or perspicuity but through the crapshoot of birth. Now, however, the unsettled lands of the west offered the opportunity to become something based on merit instead of breeding. A romantic ideal, to be sure. But a powerful one nonetheless. People braved the pilgrimage out of a sense that the unexplored territories, while dangerous, were bursting with possibilities.

With the dawning of the Internet, a new frontier has emerged to spark the imagination of new generations. Like the pioneers who trekked into the unknown in search of a better future, Millennials and Gen-Xers have staked out new territory in cyberspace.

Now, you might be tempted to say, "Yeah, but that's just one more technological innovation in midst of many technological innovations. Why is this different?" As I'll have occasion to discuss in chapter 6, the potential benefits of the Internet transcend the technological turbocharge that allows for newer and faster ways to accomplish work. Through social media, social space is created, allowing participants to interact in a form of digital commons. That is to say, not unlike the post-Revolutionary War pioneers who ventured into unknown lands in search of new lives—and for the most part not solipsistic lives either, but hoping to create new communities—emerging generations see in social media an opportunity to explore new social and communal arrangements without the same kind of geographic obstacles.

For many of the same reasons, contemporary mainline Protestantism feels like it has steadily moved toward the same kind of low point as the established Protestant churches experienced in the Revolutionary War era. But there is reason to be hopeful.

So What?

In a post-denominational world, the take away isn't the *post-denominational* part. As soon as you say "post-denominational," people start getting their knickers in a twist.

- "Denominations are important!"

- "Denominations provide us with a historic identity."

- "Denominations give us great ways to organize ourselves for ministry."

- "Denominations allow us, by pooling our resources, to do mission on a global scale."

- "Denominations help us find and hire ministers."

- "Denominations hold our pensions." [Ministers, of which I am one, are particularly sensitive to this one.]

True. All true. But so what?

"Well, you're talking about giving up on denominations—like you want denominations to die."

Please don't misunderstand me. By speaking of a post-denominational world, I'm *describing* what I think lies over the horizon; I'm not advocating for or against it. I'm just telling you what I think is happening.

The question to ask: If denominational structures as we know them are heading for difficult waters, how are we going to respond?

"We need to try to stop it!"

Fine. How do you propose to do that?

"We don't know. You're the smarty-pants writing books. You're supposed to tell us."

But even if I could, even if I had the magic pill that would stop the bleeding and turn everything back to the way it was in middle America in 1955, why should I want to?

"For all the reasons I just gave you—combined ministry, global mission, ministerial credentialing, and support. Pensions, for crying out loud!"

Let me get at this another way. Mainline denominations are afraid. Declining congregations are afraid. People live in fear that one day they may wake up and something they love will no longer be there. Fear. Panic. Do something!

But the thing is, fear is a part of everyone's life. Given the way our brains have evolved, we carry around with us extremely sensitive threat detection systems. When being eaten by a hungry tiger was a daily concern—and not an opportunity for fame on YouTube–being highly tuned to threats was an enormous advantage. Unfortunately, that level of threat detection sensitivity not only isn't necessary for most people in our world, it can become a crippling hindrance. But until such time as the human brain evolves enough to catch up with our changed circumstances, nonspecific and often paralyzing fear is going to be an inevitable part of the human experience.

Part of the point of this book about how to survive in a post--denominational world is to learn to live with the fear. Therefore, I want to suggest, following Merlin Mann, that if fear is an inevitable part of our lives, we would do well to find more interesting things to be scared of ... in particular, in the church. Like what, for instance?

Field Notes

Pounding Nails for Jesus

- When the Chihuahua brain starts to fire, change is visible through the slats on the picket fence. The first response is almost always reflexive—view it as a threat. But this is precisely the time to slow your breathing and take stock of your surroundings. Once a little calm is restored, here are a few questions you will be tempted to ask. Don't. They're almost always the wrong questions in this situation. There is a time to entertain these questions, but now is not it. Asking these questions now is tantamount to arguing over what color to paint your house when it's on fire:

> How many ministry units should our denomination have?

> Should our middle judicatories have more or less power?

> Do you think if we released a "snazzier" _____ (fill in the blank: evangelism program, church school curriculum, marketing initiative, mission imperative, denominational logo with accompanying slogan, etc.), we could turn things around? (*Hint:* Using words like "snazzier" probably isn't helping.)

> Should we have committees or teams?

> Should we use hymn books or a projector?

> Could we fix it if we had a younger minister?

• All right. You've spent time looking at the historical trends. You know about year after year losses—money, members, prestige. You're afraid. It's understandable. Here's the question, though: Why not try being afraid of something other than going out of existence?

> Why not be scared of the fact that there are innumerable kinds of great, creative, meaningful, reign-of-God sorts of work out there needing to be done, rather than expending inordinate amounts of energy worrying about whether your denomination or your congregation will once again muster up the funds to support its bureaucratic infrastructure, or whether the church organizational model has a good enough flow chart, or about whether to "jazz up" the worship service? (Hint: Using phrases like "jazz up" may be part of the problem.)

> Why not be afraid of the fact that there are people outside your walls, outside your normal sphere of thinking, who need what you have to share, and that in concentrating on your own survival you ignore them?

> Why not be more anxious about the relationships you are failing to cultivate and nurture than in not getting all the organizational and programmatic pieces just so?

Make a Decision and Do Something

- You have to face the fact that if you're a carpenter, your job is pounding nails. If you spend more time planning to pound nails than you do with a hammer in your hand, you're not doing your job.

- You have to face the fact that the work of a denominational hierarchy isn't first about ensuring the survival of either the denomination or the hierarchy; it's about providing resources for people and congregations to do ministry. If you're a denominational executive and you spend more time denominating than executing, you're not doing your job.

- You have to face the fact that if you're a minister or some other kind of church leader, your job is ministry. If you spend more time doing the meta-ministry—that is, the work that *supports* ministry (meeting, planning, budgeting, setting up meetings, apologizing for meetings, trying to think up new names so you don't have to call them "meetings" anymore)—than in ministry (holding hands in hospital rooms, praying, writing, reading, preaching, teaching, playing basketball with kids, etc.), you're not doing your job.

Easy now. I realize planning and meeting and all those things are important, nay critical—as much for carpenters as for church leaders. There's a place for it in the tool kit. Unfortunately, however, denominations and congregations in decline tend to spend more time focusing on the tools than on using them, more time shopping for hammers than pounding nails. Organizational flow charts, and operational strategies are tools. They don't do any work by themselves. If you spend all your time handwringing about the tools, you're not doing ministry. A cheap lousy hammer will pound more nails than an expensive slick hammer that only gets discussed in meetings.

The point?

Talking about hammering isn't hammering unless it results in actual nails being pounded.

Example: Buildings

- Tools. Buildings are tools. They can be very helpful tools for ministry, to be sure. They can be extremely lovely tools. But in the end, no matter how much gold or stain glass or square footage in the family life center, no matter now many elevators in the denominational headquarters, they're still tools.

- The trouble is we spend an inordinate amount of time sharpening and polishing the tools we have. We're afraid that if things get any worse, we won't be able to keep our nice tool collection. What if things got so bad we had to sell our tools? Talk to congregations or denominations in decline and you'll quickly hear that one of the things that preoccupies them most is what to do with "this big 'ole building." The threat detectors are especially finely tuned when it comes to buildings.

- But how about this? How about being afraid of something more interesting?

- Why not worry about the fact that you're investing more time, money, and energy into maintaining the building than in doing ministry with it?

- Why not be afraid of the fact that rather than a launching pad, your building is a saddle?

- Why not be scared of the reality that there are all kinds of opportunities to offer your church as a gift to your community that are being missed, instead of being afraid that if you let strangers become a part of your church's life, somebody's going to leave the gym lights on, or cook stinky cabbage in the kitchen and forget to clean it up, or skateboard in the parking lot?

Give your building away. No, I'm not necessarily talking about selling the place and giving the money to the poor (though I can think of plenty of theologically compelling arguments why you might want to do that—remember the rich young ruler in Matthew 19:16–30, for instance?) I'm talking about seeing your building as a gift you can share with the community, not as an heirloom to be covered in plastic and stored in mothballs. Church buildings are hammers—if they're not being used to pound nails, they're just decorations in a lovely toolshed.

The point?

If your church building is a tool, and if you spend more time polishing and oiling the stuff in your toolbox than actually making things—it's altogether appropriate to wonder whether you are a carpenter or merely a tool collector.

- Why not be scared of the fact that there are loads of people who don't want to have anything to do with the church anymore because they've been turned off or hurt through the church's ham-fistedness (or, in many cases, worse, the church's silence) on issues like openness to and affirmation of LGBT people, rather than being afraid that if you accept and celebrate gay people, somebody's going to leave your church and walk down the street to the other church that has a praise team and catchy bumper stickers?

Love the people Jesus loves. Of course, someone might object here that Jesus loved everyone, but that he had definite ethical standards he expected people to live up to. My response: Exactly!

But it is instructive to remember that Jesus loved those who'd been God's gatekeepers in the religious arena by repeatedly calling them hypocrites and whitewashed sepulchers (in the case of the Chief Priest, the Elders, and the Pharisees) and chuckle-heads and point-missers (in the case of his own disciples)—while, on the other hand, loving with tenderness and compassion those who'd been dismissed or forgotten by the religious folks (i.e., the blind, the lame, the prostitutes, tax collectors, and lepers). The church needs to figure out how to love the latter without becoming the former. Then, like Jesus, we can worry about doing our jobs as a vocation given us by God, rather than worrying about how many people like us.

Ministry is the work. Loving people is the nail-pounding the church needs to use all its fancy tools to do.

The point?

If you make decisions about justice based more on who you're going to lose to the church up the road than on who you're going to make room for, you need to seriously ask yourself whether it's ministry or maintenance you care most about; which is to say, are you more concerned about pounding nails or forming a carpenter support group?

If you're going to be scared, why not make time to be scared of more interesting things?

4

"Spiritual but Not Religious" or Missional Rather Than Institutional

The Telegraph and Its Plunge into the Abyss

The telegraph—that was a pretty good piece of technology. In the nineteenth century, telegraphy allowed for the transmission of information over a great distance by using electrical impulses and some wires. It was an amazingly important innovation. As the world expanded in the wake of post-Revolutionary War exploration, the telegraph became "the" way business got done. It was efficient and could be pursued at a reasonable cost. The market horizon for telegraphy seemed endless, the need for it inevitable. Western Union became a powerhouse.

After some years, however, a guy named Alexander Graham Bell came along and invented the telephone. This new technology could carry not only electric pulses read as Morse code but voice. Pretty slick. In fact, Bell offered to sell the technology to Western Union for $100,000–which, in inflation-adjusted dollars, is roughly 2 million dollars (http://www.asymco. com/2010/09/16/the-parable-of-the-telegraph/). A small price to pay, one would think in retrospect, to own a soon-to-be monstrously profitable technology. Western Union declined the offer, doubling down on telegraphy as an *inevitable* technology. Seen through the eyes of the context of the latter half of the nineteenth century, Western Union's refusal to buy in on telephony makes perfect sense.

Who would need such a thing? The market for the information conveyed by the telegraph was primarily upscale. Merchants and traders used it as a quick and efficient means of sending data and information over long distances. Besides, there was already a heavy investment in the technology. What would they do with all that ticker tape? Since telephony differed enough from telegraphy, there would need to be a heavy front-end investment in a completely new infrastructure. New cables. New ways of organizing the information that flowed through the cables via switchboards. New workforce of people to operate those switchboards. Moreover, Horace Dediu points out that figuring out a way to monetize it would take a completely different pricing model. You couldn't just charge by the word anymore. So, how would you charge people for it?[1]

Taking into consideration all the perfectly good reasons for not taking Alexander Graham Bell's offer, Western Union's decision to stand pat in the face of technological innovation makes sense. In 1876, you could understand the president of Western Union saying that the telephone was "nothing but a toy"—a remark he would soon come to regret (http://en.wikipedia.org/wiki/Alexander_Graham_Bell).

We know the rest of the story. The telephone went on to displace the telegraph—not only in new domestic markets, but also taking over Western Union's primary market–merchants and traders.

What happened?

Disruption

Disruption Theory. Sounds pretty ominous, doesn't it? In 1995, a Harvard economist by the name of Clayton Christensen published an article entitled "Disruptive Technologies: Catching the Wave" (http://www.cc.gatech.edu/~spencer/courses/ethics/misc/bower.pdf). In the article, he and his co-author Joseph Bower put forward a new theory of business and technology that better tells the story of how businesses adapt (or fail to adapt) to technological innovations. The theory goes something like this:

> Company A is a small company with scarce resources. It takes existing technology and rearranges it in some innovative way. Initially, the innovation is too small and too obscure to be bothered with by bigger, more well-established companies. Company B, an industry giant, knows about the innovation, but figures it won't work, or can't spare the resources to devote to such a small project.

---

[1]Horace Dediu offers a nice rehearsal of the history of the telegraph and its eventual displacement by the disruptive technology represented by the telephone in this article (http://www.asymco.com/2010/09/16/the-parable-of-the-telegraph/). I'm grateful for his insight, on which I depend for much of my analysis.

So company B ignores the innovation.

Meanwhile, company A is working to perfect its innovation, which starts out clunky and costly—and appeals only to a small emerging market. As company A gets better at its innovation, company B starts getting worried and decides to go after the upscale portion of the market. This market proves to be too small.

Company A continues to get better and better at creating and marketing its product, pushing company B into smaller and smaller upscale markets—until one day company A overwhelms the industry titan, company B, pushing it further into irrelevance.

Does the Church Need to Worry about Disruption?

In a word, yes.

I have witnessed (and participated in) a great deal of heated debate over the inevitability of institutional disruption and its potential manifestation in Protestantism—a post-denominational world.

On one side of the argument: We ought to let the institutional church, with its dependence on denominational superstructures, die because it presents more problems than it solves.

On the other side: We ought to preserve the institutional church precisely because the denominational superstructures, like governments, provide services and opportunities impossible for smaller groups.

By way of disclaimer, I will say that whether I agree with the arguments or not, I certainly understand the passion that prompts them on both sides of the issue. I want to be clear that I know the value of the institutional church and its denominational expressions. Without it we wouldn't have (or at least have in the same way) such amazingly important innovations as hospitals, schools, aid agencies, ecumenical initiatives, and the like. I have both benefited from and contributed to the systems that comprise the institutional church's position of dominance. Consequently, I take no joy in reflecting on its demise.

I would like to suggest, however, that we name that over which we are fighting. The current debate about the viability of the institutional church is a technological one. This is important to get right, so let me be clear: The *church* is a community of people called by Christ to equip disciples for the reign of God. By this definition, the church is a conceptual truth that followers of Jesus are constantly trying to embody in particular ways and particular places. It is the "embodiment in particular ways and particular places" over which there is an argument—not over the "conceptual truth." That is to say, "the church" and "the institutional church," while they sometimes overlap in the Venn diagram, are not the same things. The institutional church, as we have known it in the West, is a technological innovation, a strategy, a delivery system. It's important to point out, though, that when I say "institutional church," I'm referring to a whole host of things, from organizational structure and culture (local, regional, and denominational) to programmatic emphases, from its status as an American cultural "player" to its role as the dominant religious voice. However, the institutional church is a *way* of doing things; it's not the things themselves.

In certain times and places the institutional church has been enormously effective at trying to accomplish the conceptual truth of the mission of Jesus' followers. So effective has the institutional church been, in fact, that for years it has seemed like the only way (or at least the only *proper* way) church could be done. The institutional church achieved over time an air of inevitability.

Because of some important shifts culturally and demographically that have led to consistent decline, the institutional church's air of inevitability has seemed less certain of late. While its dominant role has been under assault for some time (the decline of mainline denominations is but one indication), questions about the long-term viability of the institutional church have become increasingly pressing.

That the discussion around the institutional church be framed as a matter of technological innovation is important, it seems to me, from the standpoint of understanding not only the passing of certain forms, but of adequately accounting for the emotions attached to the discussion.

If you had spent your whole life invested in the technology of telegraphs, it should come as no surprise that there would be feelings of anxiety when someone announced a potential technological replacement.

- "I did all of my business over the telegraph. Are you saying my life's work was a waste of time?"

- "My daughter was married, and I heard about it by telegram. I can't describe my feelings of joy when first looking at that announcement—which I still have in a shoebox. A phone call couldn't have lasted like that."

- "We've got all these huge buildings dedicated to the telegraphic dream. What do you expect us to do with them? I mean, my father was the architect who designed them."

Or on the other side:

- "What did the telegraph ever do for me? I never sent or received a telegram."

- "I went to school, spent a lot of time and money, wracked up debt learning to become a telegraph operator—and nobody will give me a job. Why should I care what happens to the telegraph?"

- "The telephone is so amazingly superior to telegraphy, I just can't understand why anyone cares what happens to Western Union."

To both sides the comments of the other sound either hopelessly cold or hopelessly irrelevant:

- "You just don't understand how inadequate the telegraph is. I'm only telling you the way it is."

- "You just don't understand what a great technology telegraphy is. I'm only trying to give you the benefit of my experience."

But here's the thing: The institutional church is a tool, as is whatever comes along to challenge it. It's possible to argue about the superiority of the tools while acknowledging that the primary reason the tools exist is to do a job that will always be larger than the tools themselves.

Important point to remember: Tools change

(Just ask Alexander Graham Bell's industrial heirs about the prospects for landline telephony today. In fact, even the replacement for landline telephony—i.e., cellular telephony—is experiencing challenges from texting and social media to its newfound dominance.)

The Last Will and Testament

We *will*, that this body die, be dissolved, and sink into union
with the Body of Christ at large; for there is but one body, and
one Spirit, even as we are called in one hope of our calling.

—The Last Will and Testament of the Springfield Presbytery

In 1804, in the wake of the great passion stirred up over the emergence of Revivalism, Barton Stone and some other Presbyterian ministers gathered together to dissolve the Springfield Presbytery after only ten months of existence. As I discussed in chapter 2, their words suggest a deep-seated distrust of organizational structures, which they viewed as an obstacle to Christian unity.

People today, especially emerging generations, also view the church with suspicion. To many, the church represents a desperate organization that has failed to live out the compelling claims of the gospel, settling instead for attempts at institutional relevance and stagnant orthodoxies. There is more going on, I fear, than can be fixed by slick marketing campaigns or by becoming conversant in the latest trends in church-growth dogma. One of these things—suspicion of religious structures—lies outside the church's control (a fact I take to be a good thing).

While I don't claim to be a theoretician of the Emerging/ent trajectories in ecclesiology, I know that distrust of institutions and structures is one of its defining characteristics. Mainliners have spoken for years about, at least what has appeared to us to be, the deplorable lack of denominational loyalty—especially among the young. We've bemoaned this state of affairs variously as a failure of education, evangelism, and worship "style," or as the decline of clerical vocations, or as the intransigence of the Functional Church model (in which churches have organizational charts that look curiously like Jesus-y versions of the organizational charts for John D. Rockefeller's Standard Oil).

And though all of these things, and more besides, are partly to blame for the rapid decline of mainline denominations as the cultural "cool kids," the fact remains that even were we to get all of these things right (whatever *that* means), it is by no means a settled matter that the church could recapture its relevance as a cultural heavyweight circa 1950 (or, again, even if it did, that we should consider that a good thing). But that fact should not dishearten mainline denominations like the Methodists and the Disciples, who found a voice in the aftermath of the Revolutionary War giving shape to people's newly cultivated suspicion of religious institutions.

The Last Will and Testament of the Springfield Presbytery, a foundational document for the Christian Church (Disciples of Christ), frames an understanding of the church as less concerned with particular lines of demarcation or institutional structures than with living in unity. Disciples have long borne some latent embarrassment for taking 150 years to arrive at the denominational party, having officially formed as a denomination in 1968; but the relative newness of the Disciples of Christ may allow it to grasp hold of the trappings of denominationalism less tightly, and in the process, may provide it with something important to say to mainline denominations panicked by the thought of a post-denominational world.

Rather than expending energy in fortifying structures to organize ministry, mainliners could be devoting themselves to ministering.

The cry I hear from those people who no longer view the church as viable often focuses on the amount of time and resources the church wastes propping up bureaucracy. People are not breaking down the doors of the church in search of committee work, seeking to keep something alive they didn't make and in which they have little investment.

One of the purposes of this book is to enter an extended reflection in which mainliners can rediscover what it means to focus on ministry dedicated, not to self-preservation, but to dissolving the lines and barriers that prevent us from sinking "into union with the Body of Christ." For people formed by the crucifixion, death is a hopeful thing.

This chapter explores the ways that the anti-institutional impulses of successful Second Great Awakening movements offered a timely and important new alternative to the way church had been traditionally conceived. I argue in this chapter that recapturing the sense of mission over the urge to maintain structure is again a timely and important word in a post-denominational world.

The Rise of the Anti-Institution

The *Last Will and Testament of the Springfield Presbytery* sets the stage for a movement built on the ideal of mission over institution. But anti-institutionalism was a hallmark of the period following the Revolutionary War, not just among those in the Stone/Campbell movement, or even among those kindred spirits in the Methodist and Baptist church, but in society as a whole. Hatch writes that "this crisis of confidence in a hierarchical, ordered society demanded fundamental reform in politics, communications, law, medicine, and religion" (23). Institutions as such became a target of suspicion, similar to the institutional suspicion of the 1960s.

Methodists, for instance, which theoretically had a hierarchical structure, abandoned much of that structure in frontier America. The heart of Methodism on the frontier were the classes, which were groups within a congregation that met weekly for prayer and study and maintained an intimate and experiential feel. Together with itinerate evangelists, the classes kept Methodism democratic—similar to modern-day cell groups. Though a hierarchical system existed in Methodism, the real control exerted was local.

One could argue that the problems associated with what eventually became Methodism's episcopal structure began when itinerate evangelists stopped itinerating, becoming a professional clergy, and concentrated their energies on organizing the churches now under their control. That is to say, once the focus shifted from mission to institutional maintenance, problems arose that had less to do with the work than with sharpening and polishing the tools for the work.

Conditions were perfect for people to start thumbing their noses at traditional religious organization. The pioneers were a long way from the long arm of ecclesiastical authority. Those pioneers, having moved across the treacherous terrain of the frontier, carving out homes and towns from the wilderness on nothing more than grit and determination, were much less likely to warm to the idea of somebody, religious or otherwise, coming in and telling them how to live. These flinty trailblazers weren't naturally submissive; they demanded greater participation in the direction and scope of ministry.

Ironically, this description of the pioneers and their distrust of institutional religious authority in the post-Revolutionary War era sounds eerily similar to the kinds of concerns emerging generations articulate when talking about mainline denominations:

"What do they know about us? They're not even here where we are."

"The reason I got out of religion was because I was sick of people trying to tell me what to think about God. I don't need somebody from the home office telling me what I should care about."

"They're irrelevant. If they ceased to exist tomorrow, most people wouldn't even know it."[2]

Mainline denominations in a post-denominational world have a heavy lift in trying to convince emerging generations that the institutional church offers a platform for ministry rather than desperate clutching after self-preservation. Making the case that denominational executives who occupy offices in distant places aren't scary trolls concerned with taking money,

---

[2]I'm not saying they're right; I'm just telling you what I continue to hear. I suspect denominational officials got into the work they now do believing they could do more good for more people working in a centralized institutional setting. I'm not running down the work denominational officials do—which, again, I think is almost always well intended and often important; I'm just reporting.

warehousing institutional power, and imposing orthodoxy will continue to be a challenge.

An increasingly large number of lay people have no real historic ties to the denominations in which they are members, since they've transferred from other denominations or have come later in life from no denomination at all. To many of them the organization of mainline denominations is either irrelevant, expensive, or unwieldy—or some combination of all three simultaneously. In addition to the disconnect between mainline denominational leadership and the laity, people tend, for a variety of reasons, to continue to be suspicious of hierarchy in any form. Emerging generations—not unlike their counterparts in the Baby Boomer generation, who cut their teeth on protest, dissent, and the anti-institutionalism of the 1960s—are especially sensitive to any group organized hierarchically.

I sense, though, that among emerging generations, anti-institutionalism is pragmatic rather than dogmatic (which may explain some of the chafing between Millennials and Boomers). That is to say, my read of Millennials is that their antihierarchical anti-institutionalism arises in large part because they've never seen hierarchical institutions work. The post-World War II ecclesiastical tail that wagged the cultural dog is distant history to them. All they've ever known is decline—a decline that corresponds with mainline complaints about shrinking bureaucracy. What I'm afraid they hear from declining mainline denominations is something like: "We used to have it good. We were big and important. Something happened, and now we're small and unimportant. If we're going to survive, we need to make sure to support the institution."

Response: *"Why would we do that?"*

In a post-denominational world, mainline denominations are going to have to figure out a way to answer that question in a way that emphasizes ministry and de-emphasizes organizational self-preservation.

Spiritual but Not Religious (Part 1)

One of the courses I teach is a theory and methods course on the study of religion. Since I teach at a public university, I am explicit about the fact that I have no expectations that my students have any faith commitments. Nevertheless, when we start talking about religious organization and hierarchy, I will ask my students, "Would you consider yourself: (a) spiritual but not religious, (b) religious but not spiritual, (c) both, or (d) neither?" It should not come as any surprise that many college students self-identify as "spiritual but not religious." My students tend to be extremely positive about the word "spiritual" but generally negative about the word "religious." When I ask why, it usually comes down to two complaints: (1) dead structures and rituals, or (2) hypocrisy.

If you say, "We need to do _____," emerging generations want to know why. Saying, "That's just the way we do things around here," strikes young adults as the grown-up equivalent of "Because I said so"; which is to say, not very well.

It's a toss-up as to which of my students find more off-putting between dead structures and hypocrisy. But for the moment, I want to focus on the dead structures and rituals. I will take up the issue of hypocrisy in the last part of the book.

Making Decisions in a Changing World

In one church where I pastored, the office administrator approached me about changing her office hours to accommodate her daughter's school schedule. As a single mother, she didn't have anyone to pick her daughter up when school let out. Acceptance of the office administrator's request would not change the number of hours she worked, but would shift the start time back by 45 minutes. I thought her request reasonable. I told her that we would make the adjustments necessary to support her so she could take care of her daughter.

Easy. Request + decision = everyone's happy. At least that's what I thought until the issue came up in an Executive Committee meeting. As we were going over new business, one of the members said, "I heard you unilaterally changed the office administrator's hours. Who gave you the authority to do that? That should have been a board decision."

I said, "I didn't think I needed board approval to adjust the office hours of someone I'm responsible for overseeing."

"Well, you do. That's the way our church structure works."

"Actually, I'm not so sure it *is* the way our church structure is supposed to work," I said. "And if it is, if every decision has to be run through a complicated and time-consuming process in order to make decisions, we're never going to get anything done."

"Well, I've run a business for years, and you can't just up and change the office hours to suit the schedules of the employees."

"But if the church is going to stand out in a culture that sees people as merely 'human resources,' to be used and replaced as easily as machine parts, we need to think of this less as a profit-making business than as a ministry."

"That's naïve."

Let me pause here to say that I'm not necessarily interested in spending a great deal of time dissecting the details of this particular decision. What I'm more interested in exploring are the two reasons presented, arguing that my decision to allow the office administrator to adjust office hours was *preemptive* and *unjustified*.

The first criticism—namely, that I had transgressed the organizational rules—is a question of organizational philosophy. The second criticism— suggesting that I had made a bad business decision—goes to the very heart of the church's identity and mission. I want to spend some time addressing both of these criticisms and how they affect people's view of the church. Then I want to take a look at the practical matter posed by the opposition to my decision-making: blocking. Let's look at the first criticism. Making a decision without going through the appropriate channels is a legitimate concern. Determining who has the authority to make decisions requires some attention. If the process winds up being too loose, no safeguards exist to place a check on bad decisions. Anomie is not a sustainable organizational model. On the other hand, too many safeguards can stifle creativity and initiative. Making the process of deciding too onerous is a disincentive to leadership. Grownups don't want to have to raise their hands to go to the bathroom, and grownup leaders don't want to have to get board approval for stapler purchases.

Decision-making lives on a continuum, the extreme poles of which are anarchy and tyranny. Therefore, maintaining that healthy decision-making ought to navigate between those two poles seems so obvious that mentioning it risks insulting the reader.

"Of course, everybody knows that you can't let people do whatever they want to do, spend whatever they want to spend. Neither do you want a central committee constantly having to cut everybody's steak for them."

Unfortunately, though, I think a potential pitfall lies in thinking that the decision-making sweet spot falls exactly in the middle. Actually, that's not true: I think the pitfall lies in the fact that most congregations believe that their decision-making philosophy *already* occupies the middle ground, when in fact, the nature of church organization coming out of the Western industrialized twentieth century weights decision-making in favor of bureaucratic authority. I'm speaking on a strategic, rather than a tactical level—meaning, I'm talking not about the decisions a congregation makes, which will vary according to context, but about the way a congregation makes those decisions. To put a finer point on it, I'm not even speaking about the process for making decisions. Instead, I'm speaking about the philosophy congregations use when making decisions, the context in which decisions get made.

Now, you may say that most congregations don't have "a philosophy" about decision-making. I would argue that they do, but that it's rarely explicit, and therefore rarely subject to interrogation and revision. That is to say, most congregations don't take time to think on a meta-level about decision-making.

What do I mean?

Most young people—that elusive demographic I've chosen to call "emerging generations," who appear to have taken a pass on the church—think about decision-making in a completely different way from their elders. People from the Silent Generation (people born 1925–1945) and the Baby Boomer Generation (people born 1946–1964) grew up in a changing world. But much of that change came on a macro-level over a sufficiently extended period of time. As we've already discussed, technology changed. The work performed by the labor market changed. Political ideologies changed. However, those things all changed at a rate slow and steady enough for people to adjust.

The watchword for these generations (especially as it relates to vocation) is *stability*.

Though the world was beginning to change more rapidly by the time Baby Boomers showed up, they had a close enough relationship to stability through the world their parents had built that they had a view of the world that assumed stability as a backdrop.

For the most part, Baby Boomers were free to leave a nest that was culturally and economically anchored. Low divorce and unemployment rates made for a world in which it was safe to explore.

"Yeah, but what about the 1960s? Wasn't that all about change?"

Of course. But the 1960s were the apotheosis of cultural adolescence. Experiment. Drop out. Fight the system. Question authority. But what is characteristic of adolescence? Adolescence is a developmental stage in which boundaries are challenged—sometimes fiercely—so that identity can be established. In commenting on the cultural shift underway in the 1960s, we often focus all of our attention on the "challenging" done by Baby Boomers without devoting sufficient attention to the "boundaries" that made those challenges intelligible qua "challenge."

Stability is the ether in which challenge and exploration can take place. I can drop out and backpack across Europe or take a year off to pursue my muse as a sitar player while working in an Alaskan fish cannery, because I know that if it all falls apart, I can go home and get a job in the family furniture store. Or if my family doesn't have a furniture store, then at just about any of the other tedious endeavors I've tried so ceaselessly to escape. Even if I'm just a factotum or a ridiculously over-qualified vacuum cleaner salesperson, I know I have somewhere to land, because the world I've inherited is predictable, firm, safe.

The generations that follow behind the Baby Boomers (Gen-X and the Millennials) don't have that same luxury. Generationally, they don't have the same expectations of a stable world. Two indicators that kept the world safe for their parents have shifted dramatically for young people: divorce rates (http://www.divorcerate.org/) and unemployment rates (http://www. washingtonpost.com/blogs/ezra-klein/post/is-the-real-unemployment-rate-stuck/2011/08/25/gIQAVyiTiQ_blog.html) (especially among minorities [http://www.marketplace.org/topics/economy/unemployment-rate-higher-minority-communities]) have risen dramatically. The world to Gen-Xers and Millennials doesn't represent stability. It's much more uncertain.

Consider the exponential growth of the Internet. Back in the 1990s it took America Online (AOL) nine years to reach one million subscribers. In the 2000s it took Facebook nine months to reach a million. But in 2012 it took the mobile app Draw Something all of nine days to reach a million downloads (http://5by5.tv/criticalpath/33).

When you add into the equation the exponential speed with which technology is reshaping the world, you get generations of younger people who have no other expectation than that what is now, most likely will not be tomorrow—whether that's socio-religio-political institutions or iPods.

Being the Last Buggy Whip Salesman of the Month

The difference in generational understanding about something as simple as what kind of world we live in means that appreciating the way people come to decision-making in the church is crucial. That is to say, dear reader, understanding decision-making philosophy, the meta-level questions around the way decisions get made, can prove remarkably useful.

If you find that young people in the church are frustrated when you try to bring them into leadership positions because of what they perceive to be institutional timidity or stodginess, this may be why.

If you find that older people in the church are frustrated when you try to bring young people into leadership positions because of what they perceive to be casualness toward the institution or brashness, this may be why.

If you are conditioned to believe that the world is largely a stable place, any change is a potential threat to that stability.

If you are conditioned to believe that the world is constantly changing, then change isn't threatening; it's an inevitability.

So, if you want young people to begin to come behind and take up leadership roles in the church (denominationally or congregationally), you're going to have to make peace with the fact that they care much less (shockingly, scandalously less) than you do about saving the institution. They don't have any real expectations that the institution (at least as it's presently constituted) will be around anyway.

Mainline denominations need to quit worrying about saving the buggy whip industry and start thinking about the need buggy whips satisfy and how that need can be met in a world where change isn't the enemy—it's the air we breathe. As Merlin Mann has observed, "being the last 'buggy whip salesperson of the month' is great in the short run, but that bronze plaque is going to become an anchor much sooner than you realize."

In a post-denominational world the church will necessarily have to come to terms with the impression among the "spiritual but not religious" that its devotion isn't to Jesus but to its own survival. Whether or not it's true, one of the pervasive beliefs among those who have given up on the church is that the church spends more time thinking about how to reinforce an outdated structure than in thinking about the mission that structure originally sought to support.

Do We Have to Look Like a Fortune 500 Company?

Now, let's take a look at the second criticism. The issue at the heart of the second criticism of my decision to allow the office administrator to change the hours centered on the fact that it wasn't "good business" to cave in to the employees. I want to suggest that, at least in part, it is this framing of the church as a business that has prompted disaffection with the church as a dead structure.

The way that people interact with organizations is changing. Young people in particular assume that one's relationship to one's work is undergoing constant revision. This poses a problem to churches, untold numbers of which have structured themselves in ways that mimic the organizational models of early twentieth century manufacturing businesses.

In a post-World War II era, when the country was heavily invested in manufacturing as the life-blood of the economy, the functional church model—based on the industrial organizational model, which privileges efficiency and production—appeared perfectly natural, almost like the universe itself was organized that way. So when churches started to have a "board of directors" that oversaw the work of "departments" and "committees," modeled after the indisputable success of Ford and GM, it seemed to make good "business sense." In fact, early visionaries of this model of church organization went so far as to understand the church's work to be production, not of durable or household goods, but of "spiritual" goods.

In a society where manufacturing drives the economic machine, efficiency and production are the metric by which success is measured. Henry Ford, an early industrial innovator, sought new ways of manufacturing cars more quickly and efficiently. He "combined precision manufacturing, standardized and interchangeable parts, and a division of labor" (http://www.hfmgv.org/exhibits/hf/). It was possible to assemble a vehicle on an assembly line in which people were given single tasks and asked to perform them repeatedly without their necessarily having any larger sense of how the car fit together as a whole. This allowed for an amazingly efficient process that boosted output while keeping costs down.

As one might expect, these new manufacturing methods spurred innovation among organizational thinkers: "If we can break down the assembly of a car into a manageable number of discrete actions on the assembly line, carried out by people trained to do a repeated action, surely there must be newer and better ways to arrange the business side of things more efficiently." So, methods of business organization were developed to ensure efficient production through standardized and interchangeable parts and a division of labor. Companies found they needed whole divisions dedicated to overseeing particular aspects of the business. It just made more sense to have operations managers freed up from the worries associated with accounting or maintenance or human resources. In fact, whole departments became necessary, which did not require as a condition of completing their tasks that anyone in the department would know the first thing about cars. And this arrangement worked quite well when it came to running companies dedicated to producing cars or sewing machines or Red Ryder BB guns. But its applicability to the church raises some serious issues.[3]

The functional church model, though arguably distorting the gospel by turning it into a purchasable product, seemed to work as a tool to organize the life and work of the church. And when churches, alongside their manufacturing counterparts, were booming, organizing like a successful business made practical sense—it was a culturally recognizable form, whose success seemed to make it the only sensible way to organize. With churches busting at the seams attracting new members in post-war America, there were plenty of people to fill out the church's organizational chart. It was neat. It was recognizable. And it worked.

So, what are you driving at, Professor Pedantic?

Ok. Thank you for putting up with the pedantry, but the historical context is important.

A few significant things have changed, both in the nature of the foundations of Western economies and in the life and cultural status of the church. Our economy is no longer a manufacturing economy, and this presents a problem. Though we aren't making as much stuff, we're still training people in institutions formulated originally to produce factory workers—that is, obedient and productive people always looking for the affirmation of the people put in charge of them. (See Seth Godin's great book, *Linchpin*.) Christian ministry, by its very nature, needs creative leaders—which, because of an older model of church organization, often punishes the people best suited to the kind of innovative adventure the church finds itself on in a post-denominational world.

Moreover, the culture, which during the mid-twentieth century was friendly to the church, has since fallen out of love with it. People increasingly

---

[3]One of the issues raised in framing the gospel as a consumable product is theological in nature, having to do with the extent to which packaging the gospel as a conveniently salable commodity does injury to the gospel; it's difficult, after all, to highlight suffering, sacrifice, and death as the centerpiece of a marketing campaign. (But that's a whole different book.)

quit coming, especially emerging generations. The precipitous decline in church membership has left most churches with only fond (but distant) memories of the halcyon days. Fewer members in this case means a lack of people to populate the numerous departments, boards, and committees that we've grown to feel are necessary to the existence and operation of any self-respecting church. Churches have fewer people but the same number of bureaucratic spots to fill; and the inability to fill them causes not only feelings of anxiety ("We have to have the committees staffed, because . . . "), but also feelings of inadequacy ("Surely all the other churches have fully staffed committees"). But why do we need all of these committees? Committees, generally speaking, are themselves hugely inefficient.

In order to justify their existence and the feeling that if there's a committee, it ought be doing something, committees call meetings. These meetings—which are often convened, not because there's anything in particular to do (or even plan to do), but because it's the first Monday of the month and that's always when the Education committee meets—are often filled with hand-wringing about the fact that they can't find anyone to chair the committee, or they can't recruit anyone else to take an interest in serving on the committee, or they feel like there's some worthwhile project the church should undertake. So, much of the meeting turns to questions about what it should do.

Then, someone will have a great idea. "Let's start a _____." Everyone agrees what a wonderful and noble idea it is. Meetings are set up to plan this exciting new foray into _____ing. Brilliant ideas are put on "to-do" lists; calendars are synced. The excitement is palpable.

Then, comes that awkward point in the meeting when some intrepid soul ventures, "This is great ... but who's going to be responsible for doing all the things we've said?" Uncomfortable silence. Then somebody else says, "Well, I guess we'll need to ask for volunteers. We could put it in the bulletin and the newsletter." A sigh of relief goes up, as if to say, "We've done everything we can do."

So, this brilliant idea goes through the ordinary channels, soliciting volunteers. It appears in the bulletin and the newsletter. The committee chairperson stands up on Sunday morning before worship and announces, "We need help with a new project. We're really excited about it. If anyone's interested, please see me after church." What happens? All too often nobody volunteers and a good idea eventually dies from inattention. Morale plummets, and it will be a long time before anyone gets excited about the prospect of rolling the programmatic rock up the hill again.

In business, it's (at least) possible for people on committees and in departments to dream up new initiatives and then compel people to carry them out—a highly touted virtue of the manufacturing model is compliance ("You! You'd better torque that bolt, or you can punch out and go home!"). But in church, people can say no, or, more likely but no less devastatingly, people can say nothing.

In the world in which we live, people are busy. Most preretirement households require that both partners work, rendering one prolific source of mid-twentieth century volunteerism—namely, housewives—anomalous. Because of the economy and the vast increases in education debt, emerging generations regularly have to work more than 40 hours (which as a concept was, not coincidentally, negotiated largely by union workers in factories to help keep them from being worked to death). And if there are children in the household mix, time is even more precious.

Consequently, one of the complaints routinely made by older members in churches—namely, that the generations following behind don't seem to be picking up the ball—fails to consider a couple of things. First, working people in emerging generations often don't have the same number of hours to commit to a community organized around committee meetings as their predecessors did. If economic pressures force you to work 50, 60, 70 hours a week, the last thing you want to do is to go sit in a meeting—much of which will be spent either complaining about the lack of participation, trying to figure out what to do and who's going to do it, or discussing when to have the next meeting.

Second, emerging generations don't have the same emotional investment in the programs and initiatives that proved so successful and rewarding to the generations that came before. Rightly or wrongly, what young people hear when churches appeal for help is: "We need more bodies to do stuff we thought up when we were your age but no longer have the energy to do ourselves."

Instead of reassessing why there is no energy behind beloved programs, dropping them, and looking for those places where there is energy, the church often notes the lack of energy and then tries to generate it by appealing to tradition, faithfulness, involvement, etc. Again, rightly or wrongly, emerging generations apparently aren't interested in propping up programs they had no hand in forming. They have neither the time nor the inclination to do work somebody else is passionate about just because there are folks who feel strongly that it ought to be done but are no longer able or willing to do it themselves.[4]

Remember: To emerging generations, "spiritual but not religious" means never having to say you're sorry for not taking responsibility for someone else's dead structure.

That is not to say, however, that young people are lazy and apathetic. On the contrary, young people by most sociological measures are interested in two things that committees used to accomplish: (1) communal or social interaction (see chapter 7), and (2) a desire to offer service (see chapter 6). There are a couple of differences, however, in how emerging generations tend to view those two things. The social component young people seek needs to address a deep yearning to belong to something larger; which is to say, they are looking for engagement with a community that will both feed them emotionally (and increasingly, spiritually), as well as offer them opportunities to work to make a better world.

As a group they are savvy about social media, and satisfy some of their communal longings on-line. This also means, though, that they believe much of what used to be done at committee meetings can be done on Skype, by email, or by Google Docs; and they prefer to reserve their time for true face-to-face interaction for something other than committee meetings. Consequently, if you call a meeting and young people attend, the meeting better be necessary, substantive, and to the point, or they won't come back.

Furthermore, an interest in making a better world, or a commitment to social justice, strikes a chord with younger generations. As a demographic, they care intensely about peace and poverty, the environment and equal rights for all. They are capable of intense commitments that require them to devote great energy to causes about which they feel strongly. (It should be no surprise that exciting communal movements like "The New Monasticism" have taken hold with emerging generations). But because of the limits of time, they tend to be choosy about those opportunities to which they commit themselves. As a result, it can be difficult to convince them that programs without a big payoff in spirituality, true community-building, or social justice are worth their time.

---

[4]It may sound as though I'm insensitive on this point, like I find some kind of satisfaction in killing off cherished programs. But the truth is I don't. I am describing what I take to be the realities churches face. I take no satisfaction from the hurt that results from a lack of support for a beloved program. I'm trying to explain why that support may have evaporated over the years.

Mainline denominations—if they're going to address the problem of decline (especially among emerging generations)—will need to rethink their relationship to bureaucracy. If mainline denominations don't let go of some things, they risk communicating that they care more about preserving in amber a bygone era than in bequeathing to young people a world in which those younger generations can create something that makes sense of the world *they* inhabit.

Who Gets to Say No?

It's important when considering organizational philosophy to point out one characteristic common to declining congregations and denominations: blocking. We need to spend a few moments on the question of who gets to say no, and why that's important when attempting to appeal to emerging generations.

"Who authorized that decision? Nobody knows what's going on around here anymore."

How many times have you heard that? What's the quick response when that complaint makes its way into the life of a congregation?

"Well, it has been a while since we talked about the organizational structure. Maybe we should look at the constitution and by-laws again, make sure we're doing it right."

It occurs to me that what's at the heart of grousing about congregational organization is fear over who gets to say yes. "Who authorized that decision?" is usually an expression of fear about where power is located. So congregations spend much of their time in organizational thinking concentrating on this issue. By-laws, organizational charts, endless meetings all exist—at least in part—to rehearse the relationship between an idea and its authorization.

"I've been in recovery for three years now, and I'd like to start an AA meeting in the adult Sunday school classroom on Tuesday nights. Who do I have to talk to to get permission to do that?"

"Well, you'll need to check with the secretary to see if the room's available. You'll probably have to get board approval for that. Is there going to be smoking on the grounds?"

"I'd like to offer a middle-school class. What's my next step?"

"You need to talk to Angie; she's the Education chairperson. She'll bring it to

the committee. Then they can pass a recommendation to the board, which will vote on it."

"We've got a group that wants to use the church fellowship hall for a drag show. Is that all right?"

"You're going to have to bring that one straight to the board."

We have amazingly complex systems of authorization in place. Layers of bureaucracy that ensure no-one gets away with anything. Believe me, I understand. You can't have just anyone doing who-knows-what in the name of the church. Eventually, that will come back to bite you. But for all the time churches spend figuring out who gets to say yes, it's amazing to note that they'll let just about anybody say no.

"Now, see, I think that's a bit of an exaggeration."

Is it really? How many truly interesting ideas have been shot down in church because one person pulled the trigger?

"That sounds like a great idea, but I'm afraid that if we let those people use the building, something's going to get broken."

*"Of **course** we love young people, but I don't think that kind of thing is appropriate for Christians."*

"I think you'll find that nobody will mind … except, Norman. Yeah, he won't go for it."

Brooms, Elephants, and Blocking

Merlin Mann has famously said (http://5by5.tv/b2w/62), "Never let the guy with the broom decide how many elephants should be in the parade." What does that mean? It means, according to Mann, that to the guy with the broom, an elephant isn't an elephant; it's a source of inconvenience. If you ask that guy, he'll say there shouldn't be *any* elephants, and that you should spend your time and money hiring more broom guys. Why? Because elephants, no matter how wonderful they might make the parade, threaten to make that guy's life miserable.

"What is the purpose of a parade?"

"To entertain people."

"Do elephants entertain people?"

"Yes."

"Then let's have more elephants."

"No."

The guy with the broom answers the question about elephants by saying that elephants upset the balance. As if the purpose of a parade was not to entertain people but to make one guy's struggle with life a bit more manageable.

Of course, people say no for reasons other than just that a proposed action produces more headaches. There are any number of reasons people give for blocking:

- We don't have the money to do x.

- We've tried x before, and it didn't work.

- We've never done x before, and we shouldn't start doing it now.

- "People" will get upset if we move forward with x.

- "People" might leave if we follow through with x.

- My aunt Gladys would roll over in her grave if she knew we were doing x.

- X is just not something a place like this should be involved in.

Or, there's the all-purpose blocking tactic:

- I'm not *comfortable* with us doing x.

Any idea, no matter how good, reasonable, or promising that runs up against one of these phrases in a meeting is almost surely doomed in most churches. In unhealthy systems, blocking tactics are virtually foolproof. And the beauty of it is that almost anyone can successfully execute them!

- People who haven't been to church since the Nixon administration

- People who have never given an hour or a dime

- People who are resentful about the prospect of having to give another hour or another dime

- Even proxies for people dead, absent, or non-existent (e.g., "My grandmother would roll over in her grave if she knew that …"; "I'm not sure we should do this until we find out what Kevin thinks. You know how he is."; "People are saying …")

- I've even heard of denominations that are set up to allow people to be bussed in for the express purpose of keeping change at bay.

Bonus: The louder and more obnoxious you can be the better chance you'll have at succeeding!

The Problem

Don't misunderstand. Sometimes blocking is necessary. Prophets are often blockers—loud obnoxious people who lie down in the middle of the street or chain themselves to radiators, people who are famous for standing up and saying "No!" We need people with the courage to stand in the middle of the road and refuse to get out of the way of the oncoming tank convoys.

The question I'm raising is not whether blocking should occur *sometimes*, but whether or not a congregation or a denomination should be prevented from ever even *attempting* great and interesting things because of the threat (real or imagined) of the broom pushers, who if asked, will invariably say no.

Or what about this: Everybody in charge knows it's the right thing to do, but nobody wants to clean up the inevitable mess: "Of course, we all know that's the way it *should* be. But the firestorm it would cause is unthinkable. People might leave. Do you know how many meetings that will cause me to have to attend?"

Organizations also devote much time and energy to set up systems that are explicit about who gets to say yes. What's a quorum? How high up the organizational chart does it need to go to get authorization? How many votes are necessary? Who said you could do that?

I think organizations would benefit from spending a quarter of the time dealing explicitly with the question of who gets to say no. What kind of investment is necessary on the part of a person who seeks to torpedo an idea? Does the person have to demonstrate any expertise in the area before being able to stymie the group, or is just "feeling" like it's the wrong thing to do enough? Can one person carry the water for another person, a group of persons, a whole demographic? Saying "no" is just as much an exercise of power as saying "yes." We write all kinds of rules about the latter without ever explicitly taking up the issue of the former.

The problem isn't just that good ideas are always in danger of being shot down. In an unhealthy system, good ideas often don't see the light of day because everybody knows up front that bringing them up is a waste of time. (Think: *Senate filibuster*.) I would wager that serial blockers have killed ten times more ideas in people's heads than they've killed on the floor of meetings—just because everybody is convinced that bringing up an idea would be a waste of time or because it would cause World War III.

The reality of the situation is that you'll never do great things, exciting things, things that change the world if every idea is stillborn for fear that somebody will object.

1. Spend some time considering to whom you give the power of veto.

2. Make sure you know *why* the guy with broom doesn't like elephants in the parade.

3. Or don't do great things. The choice is ultimately up to you.

Here's an idea for a cheap bracelet: WWJASN. Who would Jesus allow to say no?

Field Notes

So what do I think we need? I have some suggestions:

- The church (denominationally and congregationally) needs to shed its attachment to any method of organization that drains energy rather than amplifies it.

    > If you spend more time talking about the failure of the organization than actually doing something, you're going backward. Do the hard work necessary to change and move on.

    > If you spend too much time researching, thinking that there's a perfect system other people are using that you're missing out on, you're stuck. There are no perfect systems. The only system you need is the system that helps you get ministry done.

    > If your system of organization makes you guarantee an initiative will work before it gives you permission, you're always going to be playing catch-up. There are ten failures for every success. So, the more success you seek, the more you're going to have to learn to live with failure.

    > If you need total agreement before making a decision, you're guaranteeing mediocrity. Programming, organizing, and ministering

for the lowest common denominator of agreement will never excite anyone for long.

> In the congregation, if nobody wants to do it, don't do it. Quit wasting time trying to gin up the enthusiasm to do ministry nobody cares enough to do. (Possible objection: "Some things have to get done, even if nobody wants to do them—like say ... worship and paying the bills." I'll stipulate that some things have to get done for the church to continue in its present form. But if there isn't anyone who can muster the enthusiasm to do those things, it's time to start thinking about changing forms or closing the doors anyway. I'll defend the assertion that if nobody wants to do it—VBS, Women's Circle, Fifth Sunday worship services with congregations in your district, etc.—there's not much point in wasting time and energy trying to manufacture the passion.)

> If you run into resistance, you need to ask some questions: Who's blocking? What are they afraid of if change comes? Decide in advance what real harm looks like, and then determine whether you're likely to cause it if you move forward. (Is *real* harm upsetting the faithful or failing to equip people for the reign of God?)

> If you find you can't seem to move forward, identify which individual or group is blocking and whether you're prepared to move forward without them. Spend some time figuring out who gets to say no. How much power do you cede to them? Think about how you can make a habit of lovingly saying no to those who continually say no.

We live in a different world. That's a commonplace almost not worth mentioning...except that, while we know it's true, we often live as if it were not—as if the church organization that met the needs of an industrial world should continue to be sufficient to meet the needs of the information society. Unfortunately, as churches are finding out, Jesus' saying about new wine and old wineskins continues to prove uncomfortably true when it comes to organizational strategies. Whether the world we inhabit is better or worse than the one we inherited is another argument. My point is that different jobs need different tools, and different paths require different maps (even, perhaps especially, if the destination remains the same).

Does the church have to be organized like a Fortune 500 company? No. But that's good news, because we've shown over the past forty years that—its theological dubiousness notwithstanding—as a practical matter most churches can't make the functional church model work anyway.

The true test of a faithful church is not whether it can produce a slick flow chart, but whether it can produce disciples who follow Jesus. How does that work get accomplished? Who's authorized to do it? And who's authorized to say no? All these are questions mainline churches are going to have to spend some time answering in a post-denominational world.

The way to appeal to the "spiritual but not religious" crowd isn't to pour more time and resources into gilding the "religious" (i.e., structures) at the expense of the "spiritual" (i.e., ministry).

5

"Everybody's Welcome Here" or Theologically Inclusive

Onward Christian Soldiers

For whatever reason, most of my friends growing up were Catholic. I listened to them talk about having to go to catechism class or about the cool young priest who just came to the parish. I went to see them confirmed. I envied them their community. They all went to church together. Their parents knew one another from parish council. They used religious words I'd never heard before—words like Lent, Eucharist, and rectory. It felt like a popular club to which I had no access. Nobody I went to school with went to my church.

Though I envied my Catholic friends their community, I thought they'd gotten their theology entirely wrong. Why? Because they believed stuff I couldn't find in the Bible. I was taught that the foremost responsibility of a Christian was to try to figure out what the Bible said and then do it. No extra bells and whistles. No infant baptism or robed priests or Lenten fish fries. Stick to the book. It was drilled into me. In fact, I was so hard-bitten about this that when comparing religious notes with someone I'd just met, it was not uncommon for me to ask, "So, are you a Christian or a Catholic?" Simple, really. I thought Catholics were going to hell.

I was into apologetics, too. One time, I got ahold of a self-published book by an ex-priest—something about all of the documentary evidence necessary to prove to your Catholic friends just how misguided and endangered their faith made them. I had a yellow highlighter. I made notes. I practiced my arguments. I got pretty good at pointing out "Papist" inconsistencies. I even tried to convert my girlfriend in tenth grade.

Despite my sincerity then, the presumptuousness of my earnest concern for everyone else's soul makes me a little nauseated when I think back on it. I had no way of knowing how obnoxious I was. I did it out of a desire to save other people from certain damnation.

The Bible, and the doctrines that could be distilled from it, were central to my life in one of the more conservative wings of the Stone-Campbell movement. I grew up figuring I had a pretty good idea of who was in and who was out. And I sincerely believed that I had a responsibility, as I learned in Christian Service Camp, to get to heaven and "take as many people with me along the way as I could."

I don't want to be too hasty in dismissing my upbringing. I cut my theological teeth among some very smart and wonderful people. I went to Bible college. I was taught Greek and Hebrew by professors who were very sophisticated in their understanding of biblical languages. I learned about the passion that captures the heart in its search for God, from people who devoted great chunks of time to a pursuit of sincere piety.

However, it didn't occur to me until some years later that what I had spent so much time doing was nothing less than preparing for war. I viewed the knowledge I accumulated as ammunition, the various arguments I had perfected as battle tactics, and the people I would engage as the enemy. In order to conquer my foe, I just needed to know the Bible better than anyone else.

Other people built their faith on creeds and "man-made" doctrines. We were sold out to the Bible. We were explicit about it, wielding it in our slogan: *No creed but Christ. No book but the Bible.*

Common Sense Biblical Interpretation, or Why If I'm Right, You Have to Be Wrong

I believed for many years that people in other denominations had gotten the Christian faith pretty well twisted up. And it wasn't just that other denominations had mistaken ideas; it was that they had *sinfully* mistaken ideas. I believed that reading the Bible required nothing more than an understanding of Greek and Hebrew and a little common sense, and that its truths were available to everyone who read it without prejudice. It never occurred to me that my interpretative strategy carried its own

Enlightenment prejudices—or even that I *had* an interpretative strategy, let alone Enlightenment prejudices. I just thought that that was the correct way to read Scripture. An implicit assumption of a "common sense" view of interpreting Scripture is that anyone who arrives at different conclusions from you has somehow gotten it wrong; the "it" being what God clearly wanted human beings to understand. The whole thing seemed plain to me.

I found out later in my education about the law of noncontradiction: *A* cannot simultaneously be *non-A*. That is to say, if I'm right and you disagree with me, you can't also be right. One of us has to be wrong. And my working assumption was that, since I read the Bible commonsensically, the person who is wrong in this situation is you.

It occurs to me now that our stress on common sense biblical interpretation sounds almost credal in its certainty.

"Um, excuse me. You can't wear green socks in here."

"Why not?"

"It's the Lord's house."

"I'm not following."

"In our tradition, green socks are a sign of disrespect to the God who created the earth green."

"Where does that come from? I'm pretty sure it's not in the Bible."

"Well, it's our reading of the Höckenstengel creed, produced at the council of the same name in 1737."

"But see, from where I sit, that sounds arbitrary ... and well, frankly, made up."

"Please don't say that too loudly. We've just come through a serious fracas with the no-blue-socks-wearing schismatics, and we really don't need another round of sock wrangling."

"Blue socks?"

"For the sky."

"Yes, of course."

"So, if you're willing to take off your green socks and acknowledge God's <u>true</u> will, we'd be happy to have you commune with us. Oh, and lose the chin beard. God created the billy goats. You understand."

Ironically enough, I grew up in a tradition—variously called "Disciples of Christ," the "Stone-Campbell movement," or the "Restoration movement"—which was born in the early nineteenth century amid claims that Christianity had gotten sidetracked with the broad range of credal formulations. Our founders said things like:

- "No creed but Christ; no book but the Bible"
- "Not the only Christians, but Christians only"
- "In essentials, unity; in nonessentials, liberty; but in all things, charity."

The Second Great Awakening helped already established movements like the Baptists and the Methodists find a particularly compelling voice for the new realities of a frontier shaped by the American Revolution. Moreover, it made space for new movements like the Shakers, the Mormons, and the Disciples of Christ to spring up and find a foothold. In fact, the evangelical revivalism that fueled the growth of these movements emerged as "by far the dominant religious movement of the period" (Ahlstrom, 475).

The Disciples of Christ gave expression to the growing distrust of authority, particularly that brand of authority they considered "man-made." It was one thing, early Disciples figured, to have God tell you to do something in the Bible. It was an entirely different thing to be told to do something because some really important religious people said you were supposed to do it.

Early Disciples were animated by two often-competing impulses: Christian unity and the quest to return the church to reliance upon the Bible as the only legitimate rule of faith. It's this latter impulse I want to focus on for a moment.

We're a New Testament Church

Some thousands thus are dup'd and led,
　　　By prejudice and priestcraft fed,
Who love to hold contention;
　　　Their old confessions they defend,
　　　For human rules do strong contend,
　　　The ground of much dissention.
　　　Is this religion? God forbid.
　　　The light within the cloud is hid,
　　　My soul be not deceived;
　　　The Great Redeemer never told
　　　The priests to separate his fold,

And this I've long believed.
I love religion—do declare,
That peace and lover are ever there,
And universal kindness;
The Bible is my rule for this,
It points me to eternal bliss,
Dispels Sectarian blindness.
Let Christians now unite and say,
We'll throw all human rules away,
And take God's word to rule us;
King Jesus shall our leader be,
And in his name we will agree,
The priests no more shall fool us.

—Joseph Thomas, (in Hatch, 242-43)

As Presbyterians, Thomas Campbell and his son, Alexander, had found themselves caught up in the many intramural squabbles Presbyterians engaged in at the dawn of the nineteenth century. Thomas Campbell identified as an Old Light Anti-Burgher Seceder Presbyterian. Each of those qualifiers, of course, implies an opposite alternative: New Light Anti-Burgher Seceder Presbyterian, Old Light Burgher Seceder Presbyterian, Old Light Anti-Burgher Non-Seceder Presbyterian, New Light Burgher . . . you get the point. These ways of distinguishing and naming one's particular loyalties were doctrinal differences, not necessarily rooted in Scripture, but in credal formulations or in local political disputes. Such fine distinctions grew wearisome to people like the Campbells, who had had occasion to be on the receiving end of the ire prompted by occupying the "wrong" side of these contentious issues.

The Campbells began to resent being told that they must revise their theological commitments if they were to be adjudged "orthodox." They bridled at the notion that orthodoxy depended upon hewing to particular doctrines, the support for which came not from a perspicuous reading of the Bible but from the partisan wrangling of human beings who were expressing less the indispensable matters of faith than the partisan biases of local custom and tradition.

The Campbells began to argue for an orthodoxy that depended not on what they considered the "human formulations" found in "man-made creeds," but only on that which could be demonstrated as having foundation in Scripture. That is to say, you can't require or prohibit behavior or belief that can't be explicitly found in and argued from Scripture. In other words, if the Bible *doesn't* say it, you don't *have* to believe it.

Restorationism, which had historical precedence among the Hussites and the Anabaptists, represented the struggle against the institutionalized power of the established church (Catholic as well as Protestant), which had always been able to regulate belief in extra-biblical ways. That is to say, going back to the Bible as the only rule of faith leveled the ecclesiastical playing field by arguing that the ability to understand how God wanted faith to play out came from an ability to read the Bible (which is to say, from God), and not from the sniffy directives of a collection of middle-aged (mostly European) men.

The Enlightenment emphasis on humanity's ability to employ reason shows up among the early Disciples' strategy for biblical interpretation fully dressed and ready to play. The assumption was that humans—fully rational beings by design—were endowed with good enough sense to read and understand God's mind on things, which had been revealed once and for all in Scripture. God made God's will clear in print and didn't need a host of ecclesiastical factotums making up new stuff on the fly.

In effect, Disciples made a great deal of theological hay by taking Luther and Calvin even further and saying that *sola scriptura* means just that— the Bible only. The leaders of the Protestant Reformation railed against the Catholic Church's penchant for conjuring up binding doctrines that had no Scriptural foundation. However, the charge made by early Disciples was that the spiritual and denominational heirs of the Protestant Reformers had done exactly the same thing with the publication of their various confessions and their insistence on remaining faithful to the creeds produced by the Ecumenical Councils in the early church (viz., Nicaea, 325 CE; Constantinople, 381 CE; Ephesus, 431 CE; Chalcedon, 451 CE; Constantinople, 553 CE; Constantinople, 680 CE; and Nicaea, 787 CE). From the perspective of the early Disciples, the Reformers weren't prepared to throw out *all* Catholic doctrine and tradition that came from creeds and councils, especially the historic Ecumenical Councils. Moreover, they retained an unhealthy attachment to "man-made" doctrines by developing a new set of them. The only difference, according to Disciples, was that these new credal formulations had a Protestant flavor rather than a Catholic one. In short, as the early Disciples saw it, the Lutheran *Augsburg Confession* and the Reformed *Westminster Confession* only shifted the rules-makers from Catholic to Protestant. The reason there was so much division in Christianity, according to early Disciples, was because the church had fallen into the bad habit of confusing human opinion with divine will. The only way to solve this problem, they reasoned, was to make human opinion non-binding.

Interestingly, though, despite the disgust evinced by Thomas and Alexander Campbell at the prevalence of creeds among the denominations—which often found the Campbells at odds with other Christians, since not many initially agreed with them—they remained convinced that in restoring the Bible, they had stumbled upon the only true path for Christian unity. Ironically, the early Disciples believed that their often partisan disputes, on behalf of restoration and against denominational creeds, offered the promise of reuniting all Christians again under one banner. The stress on a return to a reliance solely on the Bible in general, and the New Testament in particular, as the only rule of faith was done largely in the service of uniting Christians. Barton Stone, the other (and unfortunately, too often less celebrated of the Stone-Campbell movement) famously said that Christian unity is our "polar star." That is to say, underneath this emphasis on restorationism lay the conviction that the fracturing of the church was an indisputable blight on the body of Christ. As Kenneth Teegarden, former General Minister and President of the Christian Church (Disciples of Christ) said, "The ideal of Christian unity is to Disciples of Christ what basketball is to Indiana, hospitality is to the South, and nonviolence is to the Quakers."[1]

America, which inherited many of the ecclesiastical divisions from Europe, became an even more fertile ground for new divisions. Indeed, Ahlstrom suggests that it was the "evangelical ferment" set loose in the Second Great Awakening that "frequently did stimulate their formation" (Ahlstrom, 473).

Interestingly, though Barton Stone was instrumental to the "evangelical ferment" through his participation in the Cane Ridge Revival, he found the sectarianism of denominations heartbreaking. It was the occasion of seeing ministers from different denominations sharing the preaching duties that, among other things, excited Stone about the potential of revivalism. He saw the division within the body of Christ to be sinful, just to the extent that it was an embarrassing admission to the rest of the non-Christian world that Christianity was unable to reach intramural agreement about the truth. How then could Christians presume to share "good news" with anyone else?

Part of the ecumenical identity of Disciples was encoded in its ecclesiastical DNA in the struggle over what to name this new movement. Alexander

---

[1]Kenneth Teegarden, *We Call Ourselves Disciples* (St. Louis: The Bethany Press, 1959), 36, as cited in Mark Tolouse, *Joined in Discipleship* (St. Louis: Chalice Press, 1997), 73.

Campbell liked "Disciples," while Barton Stone, Thomas Campbell, and Walter Scott preferred "Christians." And though part of the attractiveness of using these two designations stemmed from a desire to use "Bible names for Bible things," an equally important concern was that "Disciples" and "Christians" were the least sectarian options. The names of other denominations, because they referred to distinctive practices or ecclesiological idiosyncrasies, set each one apart from the others. Mark Toulouse points out that "though the concern to restore primitive Christianity was common to many different groups during this time period, only the early Disciples emphasized the accompanying belief that the apostolic witness demanded unity among all Christians" (Toulouse, 80). In other words, Disciples understood themselves to be offering a gift to the larger body of Christ—an opportunity to find a path to the unity that Christ names in his farewell prayer in John 17.

Unfortunately, however, this path led through the thicket of the Restorationist common sense interpretation of the Bible. In a postmodern world, the belief that it is possible for people to shed their prejudices, as Alexander Campbell encouraged, appears naïve. In fact, while many within the Stone-Campbell movement have given up on the dream of restoring the New Testament church through a common understanding of Scripture, there are those who have clung tenaciously to the idea that unity should still be our "polar star."

As the twentieth century dawned, historical criticism of the Bible saw a group of Disciples having given up on the idea that a simple common sense reading of the Bible is possible. Faithful interpretation of Scripture, modernists within the Disciples came to understand, takes much more than goodwill and the suspension of one's prejudices. Suspending your prejudices is like trying to look at your face without a mirror: you can never occupy a perspective that allows you enough distance to see what you really look like. You can't get outside yourself far enough to look back into your own eyes.

Consequently, any understanding of how the church ought to be structured that relies for its intelligibility on people coming to a common agreement on what the Bible says is doomed from the start—because practically, if not theoretically, we know it doesn't work. People, no matter how hard they try, bring their prejudices with them when they seek to interpret the Bible—their past experiences, their level of knowledge about the world in which the Bible unfolds, the bad burrito they ate for supper last night. All these things militate against a common sense reading of Scripture, and therefore of a common understanding about how the Scriptures say the church ought to look.

As a result of this dawning awareness that there is no easy path to unity that leads through an agreement on what the Bible says, some within the Stone-Campbell movement gave up on the idea of restoring the New Testament Church. These Disciples did not, however, give up on the idea of unity, which stoked their enthusiasm for serious ecumenism in the twentieth century.

Emerging Generations and Different Religions

When I teach *Introduction to World Religions*, I begin the class by asking the question: Why would a state-funded university allow—let alone promote—a class on religion? What does the university think is at stake in teaching you about other people's faith and practice? The students usually nail it right out of the gate: "Well, because we know people of other faiths, and knowing what they believe is supposed to help us get along."

"Right," I say. "When I was your age, I had never met a Hindu person. There wasn't a heavy concentration of them in Grand Rapids, Michigan. I'd only met one Jew, a teacher in my middle school. I was fortunate enough to have two hippie holdovers from the 1960s—Mick and Herbie—who both looked like John Lennon during the Yoko Ono period, practiced Zen, and drove a VW Microbus. Other than that, however, it was Catholics, Presbyterians, Methodists, Pentecostals, Baptists, Reformed, the odd Episcopalian, and us—the Christians."

The big battle for me growing up was coming to the conclusion that people from other denominations were Christians too—a kind of practical ecumenism. Emerging generations have grown up in the aftermath of Vatican II and the great ecumenical initiatives of the 1960s. By and large, they don't have much problem allowing that Methodists and Catholics occupy different branches of the same family tree. To them, interdenominational squabbles make little sense. They're often trying to figure out whether or not the lines drawn between different *religions* are even worth honoring.

"Aren't we all saying just the same thing, but in different ways?"

My answer is no. All religions aren't all saying just the same thing but in different ways. We have to be careful about religious imperialism, colonizing the purpose and language of other faiths by communicating that they're all pretty much the same as we are; they just don't realize it. We have to extend people respect by not implying that we know better than they what they're all about.

Notwithstanding the often-too-easy shaving off of religious particularity, emerging generations don't see the faith of other religions as threatening their own. The heroic battles in the past few generations among mainline denominations to achieve ecumenism in many ways has been practically achieved—not so much by top-down agreements hammered out by denominational executives, but in grassroots ways by local ministerial organizations and community ministries.[2]

The upshot of all this ecumenical success is that, for emerging generations, the question about whether Methodists and Catholics are all going to heaven is no longer particularly interesting. Instead, they tend to assume that the theological differences between denominations are minor matters of taste and style. The real issue they find compelling is how they can relate to people whose beliefs and practices appear odd and different, but who they assume are all climbing the same religious mountain.

The Language of Faith in a Post-Denominational World

In a post-denominational world the questions people are dealing with center less on whether "my denomination" will survive than on the emerging awareness that there are different religions all around. This raises the question: Why should I consider *my* faith special? The answer to that question might very well be an easy universalism that homogenizes all religions, asserting that they're all "pretty much the same thing." Another way of answering that question, however, could be to say that the diversity of religions requires a kind of respect for diversity that is more than a passing hat tip toward the well-worn cliché that "all religions are saying mostly the same thing."

This kind of appreciation of diversity takes work. We must take seriously what it is that each religion is trying to say, because we no longer assume everyone is saying the same things but are merely using different ways of expressing themselves. On the other hand, the study of the various religions shows that they give answers to many of the same questions. This is as true of non-Christian religions as it is of Christian denominations and traditions. So there exists similarity among diversity, and this is critical when it comes to understanding one another. I'd like to explore this for a moment.

Let's consider what metaphor we might use to explain the understanding that different faiths are trying to answer many of the same questions. In

---

[2]I want to be careful not to be misunderstood. I'm not suggesting that high-level ecumenical agreements made by denominational representatives were unimportant; they helped shape an official understanding of the relationship of the theological gifts brought by each denomination. I *am* saying, however, that the cultural shift in attitude toward ecumenism has ultimately been realized on a local and not a national level.

my lower level religion classes, I get at this by asking if any of the students speak a language other than English. I then take those students who've raised their hands and ask them to come to the front of the class. I give them chalk and ask them to translate a simple phrase—"I can read a book"—into the other language.

Afterward, I ask them each to read the sentence they've just translated. I always have someone who will do Spanish ("Puedo leer un libro"), and then usually French ("Je peux lire un livre") or German ("Ich kann ein buch lessen"). You know, the "easy ones." But then I'll get some interesting ones: Arabic, Korean, Croatian, Farsi, Japanese, Hindi, or Urdu. We're always amazed to see the peculiar-looking characters and to hear the exotic cadences. How could somebody who's so "normal looking" know something so odd and beautiful? My students clap for this lit bit of virtuosity.

Then, I'll pose the question, "Which one of these languages is better?" Confusion.

I wait.

Nothing.

I wait.

More confusion.

Finally, I'll say, "Ok. Let's try a different question: Which language is more beautiful?"

This time some brave student will say "French," or perhaps one of the exotic languages. For the most part, though, the students sit in silence, uncomfortable passing judgment on the superiority of one language over another.

So I'll say: "The most common sense response to those questions is something like: 'Those are stupid questions.'" Why are they stupid questions, though? It's because we generally don't evaluate languages with those particular kinds of qualifiers.

I then suggest that we are going to use language as the primary metaphor for talking about different religions. Of course, I try to make the point that all these languages aren't just the same thing with different words. In fact, each of these languages—because of the grammar and syntax, not to mention the culture that is expressed (and often, made intelligible) by these languages—are able to create new ways of thinking, new ways of relating to the world—and that despite the fact that they all are attempts to communicate some very common human experience of the world.

Generally speaking, my students get that right away, because it is in accord with the way they're used to seeing the world. They recognize a certain amount of difference between languages that isn't merely ornamental; new languages are able to create new thoughts and concepts. On the other hand, in many ways they are trying to organize experience of the existing world through words.

In a post-denominational world the church should be thinking less about ways of proving its superiority to other religions and more about teaching followers of Jesus to recognize the beauty in the way the languages of other religions are arranged.

"But that sounds like you're saying that all religions are equal, which is what I thought you said you weren't going to do. Isn't that just cultural relativism?"

When I encourage the church to come to some familiarity with other religions for the purposes of appreciating them, I realize that it may sound like I'm just saying that they're basically all the same thing—so it doesn't matter which one you choose. But if we're talking about language, then choice is much less a factor on the front burner.

"What do you mean?"

We don't choose our native language; it's a gift we inherit. In my case, the literal language I learned as a child was English, the language of faith I learned was Christian, and the dialect was Stone/Campbell. Now, I may choose another language later as better suited to the life I'm living, but my understanding of life, its purposes and responsibilities, has been shaped by the world made possible through the language I learned as a child.

Learning to speak a new language can be done with great time and effort, but unlearning the language that brought you through puberty and set you on a path to adulthood, the language you taught your own babies and sought to perfect for your own use as a participant in the game of life, is impossible.

Even if your concern is to get everybody to speak your language, you certainly won't be aided in that enterprise by the attitude that every other language is inferior, and therefore, dangerous.

Emerging generations, who often begin from the premise that all religions are basically the same, will not find an attitude of competition between religions attractive. At least part of the reluctance to tout one religion over the others has to do with the fact that, with an increasingly diverse population, emerging generations have grown up with people whose religions differ. They have friends who are Jewish, Hindu, and Muslim. And the thought that the church might be naming their friends as among "the lost" strikes them as "judgmental"—a particularly odious term to Millennials and Gen-Xers. Notice, I haven't made any case about either the legitimacy of the charge that people of other religions are lost or the reaction against this charge by young people as judgmental. So far, all I've said is what young people typically hear when the talk ranges to other religions. From the church they hear "judgmental." I'm not saying (although I think a case can be made for it) that you shouldn't consider your faith commitments "the way." I'm merely making the observation that if you do, you're increasingly going to find emerging generations reluctant buyers.

The reason, I think, that my students respond positively to language systems as a metaphor for religion is that it gives them a way to name differences while still searching for what's most compelling, most beautiful about the faith of others. In other words, it helps them to be serious about what others believe without having to feel the familiar pull of judgmentalism.

Judgmentalism—the New Heresy

The issue is broader than whether or not the church thinks Buddhists are going to heaven. Emerging generations find any kind of judgmentalism off-putting. Consequently, they tend to seek the broadest possible parameters for what previous generations would call *orthodoxy*.

It should be pointed out that some of what passes for nonjudgmentalism is simply an unspoken social contract in which I promise to keep my nose out of your business if you agree to keep your nose out of mine. I want to be clear that I'm not suggesting mainline churches should approach faith and morality as a laissez faire proposition in which the church, to avoid appearing judgmental, agrees to keep its mouth shut about important matters. What I am suggesting, however, is that no matter how the church *feels* about being labeled judgmental, it would benefit mainline churches to think carefully about the way they come across.

Growing up as a religious conservative (an Evangelical, I would have said), I took it as an article of faith that salvation was like an obstacle course. Once you began to move toward the goal, you couldn't go back, and every step was a potential hazard, threatening to disqualify you from finishing.

I was convinced that having the right beliefs about God was of equal importance with doing the right thing. In fact, having the wrong belief might be even more problematic than *doing* something wrong. If you screwed up and said "Dammit!" because you bent your dad's driver trying to hit rocks in the backyard, you could always repent and ask forgiveness. Wrong belief, on the other hand, assumed a kind of intentionality, a willfulness that was much more difficult to recover from. You couldn't *accidentally* believe in evolution or that the Bible might contain some mistakes in it.

Additionally, I believed that among the barriers Christians must negotiate on the obstacle course of salvation, the need to "save" other people was a high priority. If you observe a toddler wandering into the middle of a busy intersection, you have a responsibility to try to protect the child from being hit by a bus. Looking the other way is a sin of omission. In the same way, if you see someone boarding the express train to perdition, you have a responsibility to help jerk them back onto the platform. Not to do so is to have saddled yourself with the responsibility for someone else's damnation. If you get enough of those lost souls in your column, the sheer weight of them might just drag you down, too.

Now, I'm willing to admit that my description of my childhood beliefs doesn't necessarily represent all of Evangelical Christianity. However, they were *my* beliefs, and they are often the same things I hear people describe as "what Christians believe." It's important to name the reality that "Evangelical Christianity" has largely become a placeholder for "Christianity" in our culture.

That Christianity has become known by many people more for its beliefs than for what it actually does is problematic for the church in an emerging world. Part of the way I read the common charge against the church as "judgmental" has to do with the conviction on the part of emerging generations that Christians tend to believe more than they actually live.[3]

---

[3]I'm aware that *lex orandi, lex credendi, lex vivendi* is the traditional confession—that is, the way we worship shapes what we believe and how we live. Worship, belief, and life are all inexorably linked. Consequently, you can't just say, "It doesn't matter what you believe, as long as you live faithfully." For one thing, that would be (gasp!) a Protestant heresy against *sola fide*. More importantly from my perspective, however, is the fact that you can't long sustain moral behavior unsupported by conviction. So, *what* you believe (or don't believe) is important. What I'm arguing here, though, is that a common view of Christians is that the converse doesn't necessarily hold. That is to say, it appears possible to hold a set of beliefs indefinitely that are unsupported by a commitment to embodying them in your life—a fact that emerging generations in particular are quick to pick up on.

That fact, turned back upon the individual, is *hypocrisy*, as I will discuss in chapter 7—that is, "I believe this, but I don't think that means I actually have to make it a part of my life." Turned outward, however, that conviction about believing more than you're willing to live often expresses itself as *judgmentalism*—that is, "I believe this (and I'm right); and therefore, I'm holding you responsible for living up to my expectations."

Hint: The combination of hypocrisy and judgmentalism is deadly for the church, since it communicates an inordinately high opinion of oneself and one's abilities to determine what's right—an opinion of oneself that isn't mapped onto reality, and therefore, need not be taken seriously by the individual.

At the heart of the criticism of judgmentalism lies an accusation that Christians feel themselves superior. In other words, when people look at the church what they see is a collection of overweening know-it-alls who assume that everyone is breathlessly awaiting a word about how to improve themselves. Any deviation from "Christian expectations," these observers believe, must be met with moralizing opprobrium from those who "know the mind of God." Christians, on this reading, have nothing better to do than to think up rules for everybody else to follow—then set about in earnest being exceedingly disappointed in everyone else when the moral revival doesn't take shape.

"That's not fair. I think people ought to live right, but I'm not the judgmental person you so sarcastically describe."

In the absence of information to the contrary, I'm perfectly willing to concede that that's not a fair description of you. I don't even know you, after all. That's not the point, though. The people who believe you're judgmental probably don't know you either. As far as they're concerned, if you're a Christian, they already know as much as they need to know about you.

Among emerging generations, "Christian" is metonymous with "judgmental." For many people the sentence "Derek is a Christian" is a shorthand way of communicating that "Derek is judgmental," since "Christian" is merely a placeholder for "judgmental." Whether it's true or not, the perception is, for my purposes, what matters.

Why is it the perception that matters? Because, as a very wise man once told me, "The difference between reality and perception is that reality changes." If you want perception to change, you must work not only on the reality but also on the perception. Not only must the church adopt a positive understanding that it is called to *be* something for the world not just believe something *about* the world, but it must do so in a way that communicates its own humility.

Field Notes

In a post-denominational world the church has to quit coming off as a schoolyard bully, ready to thrash all religious comers. The kind of generosity of spirit and the conviction that unity is its own best marketing must drive mainline denominations to rethink what success might look like in relationship to other religions.

Does success mean driving all other religions out of business and convincing everyone in the world that Christianity is the only game in town?

Which version of Christianity ought to prevail?

How about This? (Practical Ideas)

- First and foremost: Try finding motivation for what you do in how you appear to people who aren't already on the rolls. What do I mean? Struggle to live like Jesus so that people who appreciate Jesus, but who hate the church, will see Jesus and not just somebody trying to impress other Jesus followers.

- Try seeking out community partnerships, not just with traditional ecumenical partners, but with interfaith partners. Find out areas of common concern and join forces with the Jews, the Hindus, the Muslims. Do justice work together, but just as importantly, make friends.

- Make friends. Find out about people who are different from you, not so you can figure out how to make them like you, but so you can enjoy them for who they are. People can smell a conversion encounter from a mile off; emerging generations can smell them from two miles off. Here's the thing: If you're open, you may find out that the person with the greatest need to change is you.

- Partner with a local community college or university to offer World Religion classes—not for the purposes of showing where everybody else is wrong, but because you're genuinely interested in finding out what other people believe, as well as that which makes them passionate about their faith.

- Don't enter every encounter with another person or another group believing that you already know the questions they're asking, and being prepared to offer the benefit of your wisdom. (Actually, this is more commonly known as "acting like a grownup.")

- The point of telling people about what you believe is self-revelation, not beating your "opponent" into submission. Faith isn't a competition, where for you to win, everyone else has to lose. Engaging in this kind of behavior only reinforces the stereotypes emerging generations hold about religion-as-jerk-assembly-line.

- For denominations: Figure out how to communicate your denomination's perspective on the gospel so that what gets highlighted is the gospel, not your perspective. Mainline denominations have wonderful gifts to bring to the conversation, but if it feels like you're just re-packaging old slogans and talking points, you're wasting your time.

6

"Just a Minute, I Have To Update My Status" or Technologically Savvy

Newtown, Connecticut, Sandy Hook Elementary, and Life in a Social Media World

The other day I stopped working to check Facebook and Twitter—both the boon and the bane of the contemporary writer's vocational life. As I did, I read that a mass shooting had taken place in the Sandy Hook Elementary School in Newtown, Connecticut. Twenty children, ages six to seven, and seven adults died at the hand of another young white male. Kick in the gut. I felt my throat clench. Not again.

Unprepared to go back to writing, I started looking at all the responses people put out on social media. All the things you might imagine were there—shock, grief, anger, helplessness. I felt them too.

Interestingly, after a bit I found myself going to the Facebook walls and Twitter feeds of people I know and respect to see how they were responding to the shooting spree. What I experienced was a kind of virtual commons in which people were seeking to find one another in the midst of the chaos and darkness, looking for a way to make sense of the deaths of children. What I found on social media in the wake of the Newtown tragedy wasn't an escape from the pain—though that was there too in the form of the requisite cat videos and pictures of people's lunches—but a virtual space in which to begin to process the pain. I kept looking to find words to wrap around the pain I felt as I looked at my young son, and tried to picture the faces of twenty-seven murdered people I'd never seen before.

As a way of trying to deal with the anguish, I wrote a short blog post trying to make sense of it all. I wrote it, in part, because I find that writing helps me to understand my own thoughts when they career about in my head. But I also wrote it because I felt a sense of responsibility to offer something to the conversation, thinking that there might be someone looking on my wall, following my feed to see how I was dealing with this. In an admittedly imperfect way, I tried to think and participate in the virtual commons.

You may not agree with either my approach to theodicy or my politics, but those things aren't why I'm including this piece here. Indeed, I offer my contribution, not because it's particularly profound or insightful, but because it is an instance of an attempt to use blogging and social media as a pastor—a flawed pastor, but a pastor nevertheless.

Here was my contribution to the discussion:

A Prayer upon the Death of Children

I'm angry. And maybe now isn't the best time to write—especially since I don't have adequate words to express the potent mixture of grief, sadness, and fury.

Children. Little kids in Kindergarten, for God's sake.

I'm bracing myself for the tired response from gun rights advocates. It's inevitable. Guns don't kill people, people kill ... blah, blah, blah. I've never found this a terribly persuasive argument—even on my best days. But today isn't my best day. Today—looking into the eyes of my four year-old, trying desperately not to imagine holding his little body in my arms after a gun shot has taken all that is beautiful and kind and good in this world—I can't even believe those arguments are persuasive to people who think we'd *all* be better off if everyone had a gun.

I don't have any coherent argument at this moment. All I have are the images of tiny sheet-draped bodies ... and anger. I have lots of anger.

Anger that we live in a world in which people (Sick? Mean? Struggling?

Evil? What kind of people are they?) walk into schools, stare into the face of innocence, and proceed to try to blot it out.

Anger that some folks will continue to maintain in the face of the carnage that society has no overriding interest in regulating weapons designed to kill and maim from a distance, simply by contracting the muscles in a single finger.

Anger that God watches over this fiasco in silence. (I'm not defending God on this one. God's going to have to defend God's own self, since, at present, I don't even know where to begin figuring out where God is in the midst of all this. But about the only thing I have right now is the threadbare hope that somehow God is there in the midst of it all.)

I guess that's my prayer:

God of all children, please be there in the midst of it all. In the midst of the tears, and adrenaline, and stark horror ... please be there. And more than that, help us to find you there ... with tears on your cheeks and the blood of your children still on your face. We need to know that you're there with us, in the thick of it ... where the vomit and the gore ruin our khakis, and the smell settles into our pores, threatening to become a permanent part of the way the world smells to us.

Please be there, O God. For those parents and friends who feel abandoned by you, please be there in ways that offer if not comfort, then at least the strength to make it through the next few minutes until the next wave hits. For the teachers and the police and the people who have to clean up this mess, who also feel afraid, and sad, and like they've failed, please bear them up to be able to face the horror that lies in front of them, and to be able to transform the memories of what lies behind them into something more than just raw terror and disgust.

And for us. Please be there for the rest of us who struggle to figure out how we've come to a point where Kindergartners must fear armed strangers in the womb of our educational system. Help us to find the words to put to our rage and despair, to find the words to comfort those who need be comforted, to find the words to speak justice and peace to a world bent on filling graves with the bodies of children, to find the words necessary not to meet this violence with more violence.

Please be there, O God. Please.

I'm a pastor, and part of my job is to help people find words for the experiences for which there are no words. But I don't have it in me today. I can't find them.

All I've got is a stupid prayer. I wish it were more. I wish we were better.

Writing in the immediate aftermath of the Sandy Hook shooting, Dr. Kara Ayers steps back from her own grief for a moment to observe how social media has transformed the space in which public discourse takes place (Sandy Hook and Facebook: A Nation Grieves through Social Media, http:// psychcentral.com/blog/archives/2012/12/15/sandy-hook-and-facebook-a-nation-grieves-through-social-media/). Where we used to descend on a public square or gather in churches and synagogues, we are now much more prone to seeking out our community online. From a therapeutic perspective, this tendency to congregate on social media offers real benefits. Ayers suggests that

> Facebook, blogs, and social media hold positive potential to support a nation's and a world's need to cope with the immense tragedies of today and our future. As Höttges writes, sharing grief through social media can "reverse the unsharability of pain" ("Blogging the pain: Grief in the time of the Internet. Gender Forum," http://www.genderforum.org/index.php?id=240). It can realign the poster or writer with the world."

Increasingly, social media takes up more space in our lives. It can be an obstacle to work, a time suck, a black hole of distraction (its own vortex of doom). On the other hand, social media is showing some promise of being not a replacement for interpersonal communication but an augmentation of it.

The mainline church has an opportunity to explore the possibilities of this medium as a means for doing ministry. It's free. The necessary infrastructure is minimal. And if you're interested in communicating with the generations that have given up on the church, social media offers a potentially fruitful access point.

If you're a Baby Boomer, going to hang out at the local coffee shop or neighborhood pub may not be a workable strategy. On the other hand, you can learn and interact meaningfully with young people over social media—regardless of your age.

The cost of failure is minimal, but the cost of failing to try will be enormous.

The Rise of Communications Media after the Second Great Awakening

Following the explosion of religious devotion at the turn of the nineteenth century, the logical question was: How do we consolidate these gains? It's one thing to win *American Idol*; it is an entirely different thing, however, to parlay that success into a career.

Question: How did the big winners in the Second Great Awakening sweepstakes turn their success as a cultural phenomenon into intentionally organized missional initiatives?

Answer: By combining a new take on an old medium (i.e., preaching) with an innovative use of a still relatively new medium (i.e., popular print).[1]

And nobody used these innovations as effectively as the Methodists.

Protestant preaching had retained a certain form through the years—that is, doctrinal, logical, literary. In sermons, preachers endeavored to set down the beliefs necessary for Christian orthodoxy. These sermons tended to be long disquisitions on doctrine, appealing to the intellect. In a word, tedious. The preaching that arose in the aftermath of the Second Great Awakening went in the opposite direction. Where traditional preaching used the lecture as a model, the new preaching of the religious insurgents used narrative.

The new style of preaching, as practiced by such Methodist revivalists and luminaries as Lorenzo Dow, Peter Cartwright, and Francis Asbury, appealed to common people, using sarcasm, anecdotes, wit, and sometimes ridicule. These preachers sought to form a connection with the audience that would engage the hearer's emotions. Nathan Hatch writes: "This was an age of communication--entrepreneurs who stripped the sermon of its doctrinal spine and its rhetorical dress and opened it to a wide spectrum of fresh idioms: true-to-life passion, simplicity of structure, and dramatic creativity. Most noticeable were the uses of storytelling and overt humor" (Hatch, 138). This new style of preaching broke down barriers to communication, making the gospel accessible to the common people. The religious populism of these preachers found a receptive audience. It's hard to overstate. "Finally," ordinary folks must have thought, "somebody to talk to us about God who doesn't sound like Thurston Howell III."

---

[1] While the innovations in preaching and mass print that I will briefly describe probably can't be said to be part of the immediate cause of the Second Great Awakening, they certainly helped fortify the gains prompted by the mushrooming of religious devotion the Second Great Awakening unearthed.

OLD	NEW
Educated	Untrained
Elegant	Homespun
Doctrinal abstractions	Concrete life application
Complex argument	Straightforward appeals
Flowery language	Simple (sometimes crude) language
Exalted themes	Personal examples

Not only did these preachers seek to make an emotional connection with their audience, they also sought to make their audience as big as possible. Methodists conceived an extremely effective system that took new converts and quickly turned them into preachers—a veritable American Wesleyan Amway, selling not deodorant and shoe polish but salvation. A rapid turnaround was achieved by not requiring seminary training of these newly minted convert/preachers. Instead, they learned their craft quickly by virtue of experience—something like a homiletical apprenticeship. They were encouraged to preach, and preach often. In this way Methodism spread like wildfire on the new frontier. When Francis Asbury came to the New World in 1771, there were "four Methodist ministers caring for about 300 laypeople. When he died in 1816, there were 2,000 ministers and over 200,000 Methodists in the States and several thousand more in Canada" (Noll, 173).

Not only did Methodism produce new preachers at a remarkable rate, it also impressed upon them as they itinerated the need to sell printed material (Hatch, 142). Offering each circuit rider a percentage of the sale, Methodism sent preachers into the far corners of the frontier armed with the words of salvation—spoken and written.

Among the gains of the Revolutionary War was the freedom of the press, an open acceptance of printed material occupying almost all ideological positions along the political and theological continuum. People found they could write outrageous things and not be dragged in front of a magistrate. As a result of this newfound freedom to express oneself in print, more outlets emerged to satisfy this newly discovered need. And following up on the successes of the Second Great Awakening, the new Christian populist movements leveraged those gains with a heavy investment in popular publishing. It was said of the Disciples in the nineteenth century, for example, that they had "editors instead of bishops" (Boring, 121).

This explosion in interest in the printed word transformed the medium itself. Like the transformation of the sermon into a populist medium, print began to adapt itself to the needs of a broader audience. Hatch says, "Responding to a wider democratic public, papers increasingly employed communication strategies that conspired against any form of social distinction: blunt and vulgar language, crude oratory, and sharp ridicule of lawyers, physicians, and clergymen" (Hatch, 25).

If you replaced "papers" in that quote with "the Internet," you would have an apt description of the revolution in communication taking place right now. As it stands, the Internet has taken over as a democratizing medium. People can publish all manner of content for the whole world to see, content that need not be juried by a panel of academics, that need not be limited by the attention of a publisher, or (if Facebook is any indication) that need not adhere to any formal grammatical principles. The fact that individuals have more opportunity than ever to introduce the world to their thinking also means that the type of communication strategies that ruled in a print world no longer hold. Blunt and vulgar language, crude oratory, and sharp ridicule are the lingua franca of the Internet.

Consequently, as at it was at the beginning of the nineteenth century, we are once again at an inflection point in history where the methods of popular communication have been opened up to the masses. This is a moment, in other words, for mainline denominations to explore with great vigor the potential of this new paradigmatic shift in popular communication.

I would like to take the rest of this chapter to think through what the potential benefit the Internet might mean for the church in a post-denominational world—in particular, that ever-expanding portion of the Internet known as "social media."

The Rise of Communications Media in the Modern World

The Internet occasions a great deal of handwringing, especially among those who see it as just another way to isolate ourselves from one another. You don't have to leave the house anymore to buy tennis shoes, do your banking, or research the criminal history of your daughter's new boyfriend "Snake." It allows you the sense of being an anonymous world traveler, a sedentary voyeur, or a diligent researcher…all while lounging in boxers and a sleeveless T-shirt.

With instantaneous access to an enormous swath of the world's population, fame is always potentially just an iPhone video of your sister's four-year-old away. Fortunes and friendships (especially if the deposed Nigerian dictators and amorous Russian ingénues who are snagged by my spam filter and who show up in my Twitter "follows" are to be believed) can be made without the traditional architecture of face-to-face human interaction. The Internet offers a virtual world that is deceptively easy to enter; but both its value and its costs remain elusively difficult to quantify.

To its critics the wired world only further strengthens an impulse to social laziness. To them the Internet offers a uniquely undemanding way to have the illusion of social contact, without so many of the inconveniences associated with actually having to interact with people with the kind of intentionality presumed necessary for sustained community. The natural conclusion of all this digital indulgence, some believe, conjures images of middle-aged adolescents with neck beards and Mountain Dew addictions living by the white-blue glow of giant theater-sized monitors in their parents' basement, or of *truly* desperate housewives neglecting the custodial duties of parenting to indulge secret romances with Romanian arsonists biding their time until the parole hearing.

Supporters of the Internet (especially that part of it devoted to social media), on the other hand, view the effortlessness of communication positively. They believe the interactions made possible by the World Wide Web provide another avenue to social engagement. Social media's most ardent supporters argue that the use of "social" as a qualifier opens a door to a more convenient form of human interaction that otherwise would be closed to us. As dystopic a picture as its critics paint, the supporters of the Internet, conversely, can sound just as enthusiastic about its potential to create a new Elysium.[2]

Whatever your view of social media, its presence is much with us. The growth in Internet usage over the previous twenty years is astounding. In 1990 only 0.8% of the population of the United States were Internet users. By 2011 the number of American Internet users had increased to almost 80% of the population. In the five years between 2006 and 2011, the number of Internet users increased at an average of almost 4% per year. Soon, Internet saturation will be almost complete.

The church, because of its primary character as a community, must engage this potentially new aid to social interaction. And while the church should

---

[2]See, for example, "The Internet as Utopia: Reality, Virtuality, and Politics," Joshua Cowles, author Dr. Druscilla Scribner, Political Science, faculty adviser University of Wisconsin Oshkosh, *Oshkosh Scholar*, volume IV, November 2009, pp. 81–89.

never find itself in the position of uncritically adopting every new technology or social trend, it cannot hide from the ways through which people choose to communicate with one another.

"Well, the only thing those social media sites do is give loud people a place to be loud."

It's true that social media offers a variety of opinions, many of them enthusiastically championed. Like the rest of the Internet, it can function as a megaphone for a wide range of beliefs, many of them offensive, hateful, or absurd.

But because of its relatively easy access (free—though, admittedly, access to the Internet may not be) and its being weighted toward merit rather than class, social media can also offer a voice to those who've historically found themselves on the cultural sidelines—the poor and the powerless, those who throughout history have been the easiest and most acceptable to ignore. Social media provides access to social discourse, access that has traditionally been reserved for those in charge.

Nice to Make Your (Virtual) Acquaintance

I have a friend who went through a divorce last year. Because of school and work, she moved away from her hometown. She lives in a city with few friends or social connections. However, she's very active in social media, having built a substantial network of "friends." In social media, of course, "friends" doesn't always mean people with whom we are close, but rather is a placeholder term for a series of relationships, many of which don't rise even to the level of "acquaintance." But this woman, since her local network of friends has tended to be rather limited, has invested a great deal of time and energy getting to know folks on social media. She engages them in conversation about their lives, about mutual interests, about big ideas. She keeps in close and regular contact with these people. Ironically, she would say, some of her closest friendships are with people she has never met face to face.

Consequently, when she found out that her husband was leaving, she turned to this network of friends. They consoled and encouraged her. They prayed with her and "talked her down off the ledge" on more than one occasion. In short, they loved her. They acted like friends.

Someone might argue that "virtual" friends are a pale substitute for "real" friends, that she would have been better off cultivating a series of face-to-face relationships to nurture and help sustain her. She might very well agree with this assessment. However, for whatever reason—whether because she is socially reserved, or because she has found no way to meet new people in a strange town, or because her work life is such that she doesn't have a lot of time available at hours when other people are able to get together—"virtual" friends are what she's been able to make. Social media, she would say, has saved her sanity, if not her life. And while it may not offer the same kind of fulfillment as friendships capable of inhabiting the same *actual* space, these friendships nourished by social media aren't *nothing*. And, as I suggest in chapter 8, an increasingly mobile society will continue to put pressure on the shape and structure of traditional relationships.

Because of the changing nature of our communal attachments, many people, like my friend, are going to need to find new ways of creating and sustaining community. Social media isn't a panacea for the problems associated with the isolation and detachment of a mobile world, but for many people it is a piece of the puzzle.

"But social media also drives some people further into isolation and detachment. You can get addicted to this stuff."

No question. Like any new innovation, social media raises issues about its potential for abuse (Google "Facebook Addiction Disorder"). But just because some people misuse a particular technology doesn't necessarily mean it's inherently bad. Telephones, it was thought by some early on, were going to drive people further into their anti-social shells, because telephones made it so you didn't ever have to leave the house to talk to people; you could do it from the comfort of your very own telephone chair in the hall in the front of your house. If people needed to contact others, they should just go see them—or send them a telegram as God intended.

And the Truth (If You Can Tweet It) Shall Set You Free

Beyond the potential for helping to connect people and sustain them in a world growing more and more atomistic, social media has another powerful application: Advocacy. Amplification of cries for change. Revolution.

"That's a bit dramatic, don't you think? Revolution? Really?"

Well, to take a dramatic swing at it, there were some *actual* revolutions in which social media took center stage. The Green Revolution in Iran, the Egyptian revolution in Tahrir Square, the Libyan revolution--all are examples when social media played an important role in initiating, amplifying, and sustaining real social and political revolutions.

Joke told by an Egyptian cab driver to reporters: "President Hosni Mubarak dies and is greeted in the afterlife by former Egyptian President Gamal Abdel Nasser, who asks him how he died. Mr. Mubarak answers, 'Death by Twitter'" (Goodale, http://www.csmonitor.com/USA/2011/0510/In-Libya-perfecting-the-art-of-revolution-by-Twitter).

While calling these revolutions "Facebook or Twitter Revolutions" may be a bit of a stretch—people marched, protested, and died in reality, not some *virtual* approximation of it—the fact remains that people used these new innovations in technology to coordinate action and information in ways that would have made these revolutions staggeringly more difficult (if not impossible) just a few years ago. Tactics, logistics, communication—all these are significantly enhanced by quick and easy access to social media.

"The troops are lining up. You go that way to get to them."

"But there are all kinds of people over there. You want me to go in front of all those people?"

"This is a protest. Being in front of people is pretty much the point."

The lightning speed with which information can be exchanged via social media allows for quick eyewitness reports from places where journalists from traditional media outlets are denied access. Real-time reporting, which admittedly contains its share of serious mistakes, offers a way to expand the coverage of what's being reported on by dramatically increasing the number of reporters available to cover breaking events.

In Tahrir Square Egyptian-American journalist Mona Eltahawy tweeted that she "was beaten arrested in interior ministry" (Bose, http://www.firstpost.com/world/social-media-in-tahrir-square-how-freemona-resulted-in-freeing-mona–139380.html). That tweet resulted in a hashtag movement on Twitter, #FreeMona, that ultimately caught the attention of the U.S. State Department. Within hours news of her safety had spread around the world. Othman Laraki has argued "that Twitter and Facebook reduce the cost of dissent and increase the cost of suppressing it" (Gannes, http://allthingsd.com/20110318/does-social-media-help-foment-revolution-a-theory-from-within-twitter/).

In addition to political revolutions, social revolutions have enjoyed an enormous shot of energy with the advent of social media. Online petitions, boycotts, Twitter hashtags, and Facebook groups all have the potential to help a cause or a protest reach the kind of tipping point necessary for social change.

"How?"

A study by The Netherlands Organisation for Applied Scientific Research (TNO) suggests that social media aids social revolution in helping to overcome two significant barriers to change. First, social media helps to surmount the barrier of fatalism by presenting evidence of the goals and achievements of an initiative, and by making that information easily sharable with others (Langley and van den Broek, http://microsites.oii. ox.ac.uk/ipp2010/system/files/IPP2010_Langley_vandenBroek_Paper.pdf, September 16–17 2010).

"There's no way I can aid the abuse and exploitation of Naked Mole Rats."

"That's where you're wrong! Our cause, *Dignity for Naked Mole Rats*, is already making a difference. We've rescued thousands of Naked Mole Rats from a life of exploitation—literally pulling them out of shelters, emergency rooms, and youth hostels all over the world, and giving them the opportunity for a new life. We need to add your voice to ours, so that we can wipe out this tragic oppression once and for all!"

Second, the study argues that social media can help to address the barrier of "busyness, whereby the favourably disposed majority cannot permit themselves the time and energy needed to turn their attitude into behavior." (Langley and van den Broek) Social media effectively addresses the problem of busyness by reducing the time and energy necessary to act.

"I'd love to help raise the awareness of the therapeutic effect of wearing pink socks, but I only have so many hours in the day."

"The good news is that by taking thirty seconds to fill out our online petition, you will be strengthening a movement that is crucial for our world's peace of mind. Afterward, you can take an additional fifteen seconds to hit the 'donate' button and offer a financial boost to this important initiative to shod the world in pink—all major credit cards and PayPal accepted."

What about Social Media in a Post-Denominational World?

Mainline denominations and mainline churches need to figure out how to use social media. I know that sounds obvious, given what I've already said about both the inevitability and some of the virtues of social media. However, as is so often the case with churches gripped by fear, it is highly possible—in some cases inevitable—that the wrong lessons will be learned.

When an organization experiences decline, fear becomes the default response. When dealing with the world through the Chihuahua brain, options are limited. People tend to grab for the first weapon or escape hatch they see without taking the time to understand its proper use. This impulse to reach for the first thing can be helpful in a jam. However, it's too easy to develop the bad habits cultivated in an emergency as a long-term strategy.

If, for instance, you are attacked and successfully defend yourself with a butter knife, the lesson to draw from that experience isn't necessarily to go out and stockpile butter knives so that you may now ensure your future safety. It's possible to expend great energy and expense roaming far and wide in search of the finest butter knife on the planet, believing that having found it you will be in the best possible position now to defend yourself against further attacks. Besides, going on a butter knife expedition misses a few important points.

- Unless you happen to be reading this during the zombie apocalypse (in which case, why are you reading a book about mainline denominations?), chances are the number of times you're truly under attack in a life or death situation is bound to be relatively rare. Living your whole life in dreaded anticipation of a fifteen-second encounter is a tremendous waste of a life. Real external threats for most of the readers of this book will, thankfully, be infrequent. Don't squander your life fighting imaginary battles (unless it's zombies; those are real).

- The lesson to learn from your near-death encounter isn't that butter knives are great weapons. Just because a butter knife saved your bacon once doesn't mean that it ought to be your default tool of choice. If, to use another scenario, you happen to be kidnapped by a Central American drug lord, a butter knife might help you surreptitiously tunnel out of your makeshift jungle stockade, but that doesn't mean that when you get back home you should go to Pottery Barn to arm yourself for future excavation emergencies.

- Maybe what saved you was your determination to use whatever means at your disposal to defend yourself. Perhaps it was your commitment to staying alive, and not your brilliance in using a common kitchen implement as a saber, that warded off your attacker.

Who knows? The point is that organizations are susceptible to learning the wrong lesson from their successes (and their failures).

Learning how to use social media to strengthen ministry and expand the capacity of communal interaction is learning how to use a tool. Learning to use a new tool is important. Practicing with a new tool may save you all kinds of headaches down the line. As always, however, learning to use a tool isn't an end in itself; it is merely the means through which you accomplish real work. At some point, after you've figured out what you're doing, you're going to have to get back to work—that is, ministry.

Field Notes

So What Are the Lessons We Should be Learning about Social Media?

Social media is a tool. Tools exist to get work done. They do nothing on their own.

Here's what I'm getting at. The cultural winds suggest that social media isn't the next big thing; it is right now the big thing. Consequently, there's a non-specific feeling that churches should be using it because it's the key to everything that ails brand marketing and customer awareness. So, the thinking goes, if churches can just get a social media presence, they will have gone a long way toward solving their problems.

You need to know what jobs social media can do, and which kinds of things you intend to use it to do. Social media is a tool (have I mentioned that?). It may have a lot of uses, but it's not a universal cure. If you use even a highly adaptable tool like a Swiss army knife (rather than a butter knife) to re-wire your house, you're going to end up frustrated.

"What can social media do for a denomination or a congregation?"

It Can Improve Communication

- At its most basic level social media can create more avenues for communication for those who already belong. It is often used as an auxiliary bulletin board, announcing everything from national conventions and assemblies to potlucks and yard sales. Used this way social media amplifies more traditional means of communication (e.g. bulletins, newsletters, website, basic forms of advertising, etc.).

- Used as a means of amplifying communication, social media can be both more general and more specific than traditional media. On the one hand, putting something on social media expands the possible audience. Once your announcement is put out over social media (not unlike that embarrassing picture from the office Christmas party), the possibility of it being seen increases exponentially. People you might not have otherwise thought about appealing to may come across your information through social media and thereafter find themselves wanting to know more about you.

- On the other hand, with a little technical savvy, social media can also be calibrated to make appeals with an amazing level of granularity. Facebook, in particular, allows for groups (public and private) and event pages that can carry a message to a specified audience. Having access to an easy but highly specific way of reaching people can offer not only a way to announce certain things to a pre-defined group, but, as I'll discuss in a moment, it can allow for community to develop with an eye toward confidentiality.

- The wonderfully attractive thing about social media is that it doesn't cost anything. Prior to the Internet, denominations and congregations had to expend resources to broadcast a message to a wider audience— from large advertising campaigns to a bulk rate account at the post office for a newsletter. Now, with an Internet connection and someone with a little know-how and some extra time, even small congregations can compete in the free market of attention available via social media.

- This abundance of free access, if viewed from a particular perspective, drastically reduces the cost of innovation and creativity. Because pumping something on Facebook and Twitter doesn't cost anything, you can take some chances you might not otherwise feel comfortable taking.

- Speaking of marketing your "brand," social media accounts and a website allow a culture used to "shopping" online an opportunity to check you out. I don't want to push the "shopping" image too far, since it plays into the whole consumerist idea that the church has a "product" it is looking to "sell." Nevertheless, people's habits are already formed when they start looking for a church. And rather than heading to the Yellow Pages, people (especially emerging generations) tend to go about it the way they do buying a pizza—they check online. Consequently, giving a great deal of consideration to how you present yourself online is increasingly important. If you have a static website created by somebody's cousin in 2002 or a Facebook page with 25 "likes" and an announcement about the Christmas Eve service in 2010, you're communicating to emerging generations that you don't care about what they care about—because they care about being online. Chances are, they won't give you another thought.

Side note: This freedom to imagine and create is exactly what is necessary for the church in a post-denominational world. The risk-averse nature of institutions—which comprises the nature of denominations and most congregations—handicaps them in the entrepreneurial environment occasioned by the advent of the Internet. People who've been carpet-bombed by advertising and marketing since moments after emerging from the womb are inured to the stiff, predictable pitches most church-types feel comfortable putting out there. So, let your hair down a bit.

The church has a great deal of public relations work to do in a culture that finds less and less in the church it likes. People are leaving the church in droves. Weak marketing campaigns may only reinforce negative attitudes.

So why not do something interesting? Why not break all the marketing and advertising rules and say something honest rather than something that focus-groups well? How about considering marketing a form of self-revelation and not a sales pitch?

It Can Foster Community

As my friend going through the divorce found out, social media can help set the stage for community by overcoming barriers to personal contact. The simple reason is that social media for most people is more convenient. The opportunity to communicate to a wide swath of people with the push of a button makes social media more convenient than most other ways of communicating. Let's take the possible forms of communication in the most desirable (arguably, at least) order.

- **Face-to-face.** While this is probably the most desirable form of communal interaction, face-to-face contact is often difficult to do. Burdened by scheduling conflicts and logistical difficulties, it is the most difficult form of communal communication to achieve.

- **Phone.** A phone call is often easier to accomplish than face-to-face, while still providing a certain amount of intimacy. However, a phone call usually allows only one-to-one conversation. (Yes, I know about three-way and conference calling, but most people don't operate that way). Additionally, social convention often limits people's use of the phone to certain hours.

- **Email.** Email (I'm not even going to include letters and cards, since their use has dropped so precipitously) is more convenient than face-to-face or telephone calls. People can respond on their own schedules (also a disadvantage) and without having to make a great deal of commitment in time. Email, while allowing for communication on a wider scale, also gives the sender control of who is included on the conversation. Unfortunately, email, because it is associated with "work" for many people, often carries a negative psychological connotation. If you struggle all day at work to ride herd over the neediness represented by your in-box, you're less likely to view email entreaties for attention (even from people you care about) favorably. On the positive side, email does retain some measure of intimacy.

• **Social media.** Social media is convenient in that it allows for people to engage one another without the hassle of logistical and scheduling roadblocks. It can also reach a broad array of people with no extra investment of time or resources. What social media forfeits, of course, is intimacy. And rightfully so. Reading threads of someone else's life disintegrating or the love match of the century strikes most people as voyeuristic and creepy. On the other hand, social media can operate as a convenient gateway to more intimate conversations about truly significant things. By revealing only a little about your situation, you may find someone willing to communicate with you by other, more comfortable means. The advantage here is that by sending the need to a wide audience, you have the opportunity to find people to communicate with that you would never have thought of before.

I would not want to be misunderstood to be arguing that social media can supplant other forms of communication in the building of community; nor do I think community can't be built in the absence of social media. I do believe, however, that because of some clear advantages social media has over more traditional forms of communication, the church can use it to initiate and foster community. The practical question is how this can be done.

Here are a few ways I have used, or have heard of people using, social media in the church in the service of community.

• **Loosely monitoring the lives of people in the church.** This is more practical on the congregational level than on the denominational level, but even on the denominational level it's not entirely impossible, given a specific range of people to monitor. Congregationally, though, I know a number of ministers who were tipped off to pastoral care situations just by checking their Facebook or Twitter feed. Instead of calling, people in crisis often put out an announcement on social media—believing that doing so will reach more people with the least amount of effort. Deaths, emergencies, and lingering illnesses, as well as personal triumphs and accomplishments, routinely find their way into people's status updates. Keeping an eye on parishioners can be greatly aided by social media. The same thing goes for middle judicatories and the ability of bishops and other regional ministers to monitor the lives of the pastors under their care.

- **Introducing people to one another who might never have any other occasion to know one another.** Social media can help to form community simply by putting people in touch with one another. Because it lowers the obstacles to interacting with other people, social media can create space to connect with people who wouldn't otherwise cross one another's paths. I can't tell you how many times I've been introduced to new people through social media whom my friends thought I should meet. Many of these introductions have turned into fruitful "virtual" friendships.

- **Setting up private spaces to discuss important issues and concerns.** What do you think of healthcare reform and what are Christian responses to the crisis in healthcare that prompted those reforms? How do we deal with the issue of the clash over biblical authority? How do I meet new people and make new friends in this city? We just had to put my mom into Hospice and I feel like I've failed her. Have I failed my mom? These kinds of questions can be posed and discussed on private pages on Facebook, as well as through personal messages. I receive a number of messages asking me about something the writer doesn't want to post publicly or take the time to write an email.

- **Offering points of reflection.** Whether it's a short excerpt from Scripture or another writer, the lyrics of a song or a hymn, an excerpt from the sermon in anticipation of Sunday, or just a thought you want people to contemplate during their day, social media presents an opportunity to provide material in a timely and focused fashion.

- **Connecting lay people with their denomination and its work.** Because of the rising cost of direct mail, smart denominational leaders are trying to find ways to get their message out using free media— Facebook, Twitter, blogging, You Tube, Vimeo, etc. Congregations that value their connection to the denomination can operate as a clearinghouse for information about what the denomination is doing.

Smart denominational leaders will cultivate relationships with the "media people" in congregations.

The key to using these kinds of free media, however, involves an investment in relationships. It's not enough to put announcements up on the church's Facebook wall. Emerging generations don't just want to read your digital bulletin board. Those who are looking want to be engaged. They want to see something of the church's personality. What kinds of things do you care about? How do people interact with one another? Are there access points into conversations and ministry?

It Can Give Voice to Conviction

Say a church cares about the indiscriminate disposal of candy bar wrappers or the plight of baby silk worms or nuclear disarmament. Social media can give a relatively small church a disproportionately loud voice. It can rally people, religious and non-religious, around a common goal. Blogging, Twitter, Facebook, Google+, YouTube—because they facilitate access to other people—can amplify the concerns of folks, who under almost any other circumstances would find themselves without an audience. Petitions, endorsements, surveys, and short video spots sponsored by a small church can catch fire and begin to change opinion about an issue.

I blog. A lot. I edit and write for the blog [D]mergent, which attempts to bring people together around the issue of where the church—both denominationally and congregationally—is headed. The articles we post try to help the church think through its practices, its leadership philosophy, its theological commitments and how those commitments can be manifested justly, how the church can engage emerging generations, and how declining congregations might approach transformation. A big part of what I do is agitate for change. Writing, editing, and curating a blog gives me the opportunity to add my voice to conversations I think are important. It costs me a few dollars a year to have a website read by thousands of people.

That's it.

I don't sit at the helm of a vast media conglomerate. It's just me and some of my friends taking our chance to try to change the world. Whatever I happen to be interested in can find its way into the blog—from social justice issues to organizational and leadership trends, from theological reflection to justice advocacy. I try to be consistent. I try to be fair. But most of all, I try to change people's hearts and minds.

How about This? (Practical Ideas)

- Have somebody designated to Tweet every worship service. What's going on? Why not include lines from the prayers, the sermon, the children's moment, the hymns? More people than you imagine are interested in what you do when you gather for worship.

- Have a community co-op page on Facebook. Set up a page where people can advertise what they need and what they have to give. People can barter and trade for services.

- Post short videos on You Tube and/or Vimeo chronicling what the church is doing in the community. Are you feeding people? Clothing them? Are you protesting civil rights violations? Did your youth group help clean up the city park? *Show* people what you look like, what you care about, what you're doing.

- Use your voice to help create change. Does your church advocate for justice? In what form(s)? Immigration? Healthcare? Poverty? Housing? Addiction recovery? Homelessness? Sustainable agriculture? Put your social media presence to work raising awareness of these issues. Write up an online petition. Whatever it is, you have a voice to lend.

- Do you partner with other social service non-profits and community ministries? Promote them. (This is, after all, also about building community.) I don't just mean placing a link to their websites on yours. Help them get the word out about the kinds of things *they're* doing. Send out updates on their initiatives and accomplishments.

- Try having a meeting via a hangout on Google+. With a Google+ account and a webcam, you can hold short meetings with a handful of people from the comfort of your own home.

- Regularly post links to articles that are of interest to your congregation or denomination. You can curate interesting and important information in ways that allow the people you're trying to reach to trust and depend on you as a source of thoughtful content.

- Denominations should use and promote Twitter hashtags to facilitate discussion. People want to participate. Twitter is a quick and dirty way to join or monitor important conversations.

Don't be afraid to fail. Try. Fail. Recalibrate. Try something else.

7

"I Like Jesus; It's His Followers I Can't Stand" or Jesus the Social Radical

"The Impending Doom Close"

In college I woke up most days without money. My grandmother used to send me five dollars a week, which even in the 1980s didn't go far. A couple of Big Gulps and the money was gone. Plus I had a girlfriend and a broken down Ford Escort. I needed money.

So I started going to the library to look at the want ads. I found an ad that promised to pay $7.50 an hour, minimum. The ad wasn't clear what I would have to do to earn that wage, but I figured, "How bad could it be?" I'd already worked swing shift in a bread factory, wiped down every possible exposed surface at McDonalds, and spent part of a summer in a bank of telemarketers selling tickets to the Ice Capades—all for less than $7.50 an hour.

I walked through the door at the address printed in the advertisement. It was a nondescript storefront in an industrial park. Metal folding chairs in the waiting room. A plastic ficus plant in the corner. Ashtrays on Formica end tables. A woman came through the door and said "Welcome to Cutco!" Her greeting told me nothing about the nature of the business that promised to pay me a minimum of $7.50 an hour. But it didn't take long before I learned what the job entailed. Knives. Cutco sells knives. Really nice but expensive knives. I was signing up to be a knife salesman.

117

One of the first things I remember was a sharp-looking young guy in a suit recounting the veritable riches he'd realized as a Cutco knives salesman. Then the suit guy gave a demonstration of how amazing Cutco knives are—hacking through an aluminum can, cutting a penny in half with Cutco scissors. These knives practically sell themselves, I was assured. Of course, they don't *exactly* sell themselves; there's some work required of the salespeople. But they use a time-honored sales system. *Don't worry.*

I learned some tricks of the trade:

- Firm handshake. You lose respect extending a dead fish.

- Look the client in the eye. People don't trust shifty-eyed folks.

- Say the client's name a lot. People are suckers for their own names.

- Ask about the client's family. People love to talk about themselves.

I also learned closing strategies right out of the 1950s.

- *The Assumptive Sandwich.* Act like you've already made the sale. "I can see you really like the kitchen collection. How many steak knives would you like to add? Let me get my order book!"

- *The Ben Franklin Close.* Like Ben Franklin was reported to have done, you draw up a list of pros and cons. Let the client tell you what they think are the pros, and then you understand what they value. When you know what they value, sell the heck out of it. "I agree with you that the way the knife holds an edge is important...and that's especially important for someone like you, who is obviously busy and successful—who doesn't want to have to worry about keeping knives sharp. You need a blade you can rely on!"

- *The Impending Doom Close.* Let the client know that this is a limited time offer. "There's a steel shortage in Malaysia that's going to drive the price of these things through the roof—if you can even buy them at all. So—and its because you seem like good people to me—I'd like to help you get these knives today!"

(Oh, and talk with a lot of exclamation points! Show how passionate you are about these knives!)

I tried to sell Cutco knives. I tried using the sales techniques. I wasn't any good at it, though. In fact, I really liked *The Impending Doom Close.* I could see how effective it might be. I could just never bring myself to use it. In my head I could hear the handsome suit guy saying, "Not everybody has what it takes be a salesman. It takes a certain kind of person." I didn't seem to be one of them. Instead, I turned out to be a pretty good broke college student.

Spiritual but Not Religious (Part 2)

As a kid growing up in the Evangelical heartland of Grand Rapids, Michigan, one of the things I learned early on was that God expected me to *evangelize*. We called it witnessing, telling people about Jesus. I believed in some vague way that God would hold me accountable for the people I failed to lead to Jesus through, what occurs to me now was, a kind of celestial sales pitch.

Please don't misunderstand. I'm not making fun of my upbringing. I'm not ashamed of where I come from; there are some sincerely wonderful Christians who—like the rest of us—are working their way toward God in the best way they know how.

But this whole witnessing thing weighed heavily on me. On the one hand, I'm a pretty good talker. I think I can be fairly persuasive when necessary—a quality much prized by those who take evangelism seriously. On the other hand, I'm an introvert. I'm shy. I've learned how to act like an extrovert when I have to—my job sometimes demands it. But temperamentally, witnessing always scared me. It struck me as the same kind of affair as cold calling as a Cutco knife salesman.

There was always a premium on having the right words at hand at exactly the right moment. If they say *this*, then you can counter by saying *that*—which sounds good, until you've had somebody do it to *you*. Then it's not brilliant verbal jujitsu that gives you control over your conversational opponent; it's just annoying.

"Mr. Penwell, what would you say if I could save you 50% on your monthly long distance bills?"

"I'm really not interested."

*"You're not **interested**? So, you **like** giving your money away."*

"Yes, I like giving my money away. It saves me the trouble of having to pretend that I want to talk to people who call me on the phone in the middle of supper."

Being a verbal ninja for Jesus was always a big deal growing up. Unfortunately, it felt too much like being a telemarketer—always trying to steer people in the direction you want them to go, having to be unwilling to take "no" for an answer.

It's important to point out that I'm not dismissing words. I love words. I use them frequently—every so often, even well. One of the problems with words in this context, however, is that in order for them to be helpful (persuasive even), they have to line up with reality.

The fifth step on the Buddha's Eightfold Path is "Right means of livelihood"—meaning, the way you make your living matters. In other words, if you're seeking enlightenment, there are certain jobs you cannot do. The Buddha named some: arms dealer, poison peddler, prostitute, slave trader, to name a few.

When I talk to my students about this, someone will invariably say, "What I do isn't who I am. It's my job. It's not *me*." I respond by saying, "The Buddha would say, however, that if you're walking along a certain path toward a destination, anything that causes you to turn around and walk in the opposite direction is leading you away from where you've said you want to go."

Puzzled looks. Then I say: "If your life's work and passion is to see equal treatment for women, you have to live and work in certain ways to sustain that passion and see it succeed. If your day job is as an advocate for women's rights, you can't punch out at the end of the day, and go to your second job as a pole dancer. It just doesn't work like that. You're working at cross purposes." It's much harder to separate "who" you are from "what" you do. If you say you're one thing, then having congruity with the way you live your life is an essential part of underwriting your words.

As I said in chapter 4, when I ask why my students prefer "spiritual" over "religious" as a self-designation, it usually comes down to two complaints: (1) dead structures and rituals or (2) hypocrisy.

"What do you mean by hypocrisy?" I ask.

"You know, people saying one thing and doing another."

And there it is: Words are important, but they have to have at least a vague relationship to reality, which is to say, the words and the actions have to occupy the same conceptual space. What young people want to know is: Do you actually live this stuff, or do you just talk about it?

"We live it out. We try to keep our words and actions within shouting distance of one another."

Unfortunately, at least according to my students, most religious people with whom they come in contact aren't able to pull this off. A recent Georgetown

University and Public Religion Research Institute study found that young people (those born between 1980 and 1999) are leaving the church in record numbers. The fastest growing religious self-designation among this demographic is "none" (http://publicreligion.org/site/wp-content/uploads/2012/04/Millennials-Survey-Report.pdf). In fact, while only 11% of young people were religiously unaffiliated during childhood, fully one quarter now don't affiliate with *any* religious body—a 14% increase in people walking away from religion over the course of a few years!

The church across the board is losing people, in large part because who we say we are and how we live seem too far apart. Our witness, if you will, apparently leaves much to be desired.

I think this has something to do with the way popular Christianity has interiorized faith, made faith something one *has* rather than something one *does*. Faith operates for many first as a set of feelings one possesses, having to do with God and one's relationship to God. The roots for this shift to an interior faith divorced from external activity can largely be traced to two seminal influences in the wake of the Middle Ages: Renè Descartes and Martin Luther.

After Descartes, the interior life gained the upper hand. Descartes helped launch an Enlightenment revolution of the mind. Whereas before, the external world operated as "the real world," Descartes contended that the only reliable world exists within the mind of the individual. He bequeathed the Enlightenment the "mind-body problem," in which only what happens in the private spaces of one's mind can be trusted, effectively discounting what can be known of the exterior world through action and observation.

However, Descartes' *Cogito ergo sum* (I think therefore I am) evolved, becoming in the hands of Protestant Christians "*Credo ergo sum*" (I believe therefore I am). Christians transmuted Descartes' emphasis on "the mind," shifting it to "the heart" or "the soul"—that place where all the important stuff happens.

Martin Luther, in many ways, had helped to set the stage for a shift away from the external world. Luther, or at least his popularizers, sought to replace what was thought to be the "law" of Catholicism with the "grace" of Protestantism. Over time this shift helped interiorize Christianity, divesting it of the rigorous demands of actually having to *live* like a Christian—you just had to *believe* like one.

Yeah, But What about My Personal Relationship with Jesus?

Growing up, I believed that Jesus cared mostly about my heart. Of course, he cared about whether or not I was nice. But in the end, Jesus' biggest concern centered on having a "relationship with me."

I find something very reassuring about that. I like that Jesus, this cosmically significant being, cares about me, wants to spend time with me. After all, I'm just a pigeon-toed mouth-breather from the Midwest. What possible value could a "relationship" with me have? It made me feel special.

But special is a double-edged sword. This whole "personal relationship with Jesus" thing also fed my burgeoning adolescent self-absorption:

- Jesus died *just* for me? Just so he could live in *my* heart?

- I'll bet Jesus likes the same kind of stuff I like. I mean, if he lives in my heart, my heart has to be a pretty hospitable place, right?

And though I possessed good enough manners never to say so, I got the impression that Jesus *preferred* my white middle-class life. Why wouldn't he? My life, while not courageously virtuous, remained at least politely uncontroversial.

I didn't spend an inordinate amount of time worrying about others, about whether they had enough food, or could find jobs that paid them a living wage. I never lost a night's sleep trying to figure out how to realize a world in which people didn't have to fear that they wouldn't be welcome because of some characteristic attached to them in virtue of the vagaries of birth, or whether other people could track down the kind of care they needed to keep their children healthy and safe. It never occurred to me that other people were my responsibility.

Now, that doesn't mean that I wasn't taught to *love* other people. I was. That was extremely important. But loving other people meant, at least in my mind, possessing a certain kind of attitude toward them. Loving other people meant being favorably disposed toward them . . . *feeling* love toward them. My love of people certainly required that I not actively do harm to them, but it didn't require that I rearrange my world to make certain that theirs was livable. Jesus, the one who lived in my heart, was much more concerned about whether I cussed or fought with my brother, about whether I cheated on my math workbook or looked at dirty magazines. I suspected he was grieved by the poverty and injustice I knew lurked in the world, but it never occurred to me that those realities placed any real move-the-existential-furniture-around kind of responsibility on me.

Now, I realize this is a bit odd, since my maternal grandparents gave up everything to move down to Mexico the year before I was born to establish a children's home. I spent summers living in a children's home in another country. But I believed that the children's home was, in some simplistic sense, an evangelistic assembly line. That sounds much more crass than I mean for it to sound. However it happened, whether because I heard it explicitly or because I put two and two together, I believed that my grandparents were motivated first by saving (in the grand Evangelical sense of the word) children's hearts, before they were motivated by saving (in the lowly Social Gospel sense of the word) children's lives. That's not to say that they weren't concerned with the health and safety of the children they took in to raise—they were. It is to say, though, that health and safety were secondary concerns to salvation in some larger heavenly sense.

I believed the world existed primarily as a stopping-off point, as a training ground for some better, more "real" celestial existence somewhere down the road. What you do in this life is only important inasmuch as it adds to or subtracts from the ledger that will be read out in front of the whole world on judgment day. Other things, things like justice and peace and hospitality, were important in some vague way that wasn't immediately apparent to me, except that I knew I needed to be on the right side of the issue from the standpoint of personal moral accountability.

"What does that mean?"

Let me see if I can clarify the difference in this way. As a child, growing up in the aftermath of the Civil Rights movement, I was taught that everybody is equal regardless of race. A cultural shift was under way in the late '60s early '70s (at least in the Midwest of my childhood) with respect to what was now unacceptable to believe and say about other human beings. Where ten years before there might have been a certain disapprobation about the unseemliness of using racial epithets like the N-word, the post-Civil Rights world of my childhood in the nation's suburban heartland began to see it as not only impolite but as fundamentally wrong.

On a more personal level, I knew there were certain words I was forbidden to utter—outright profanity, some marginal (and therefore questionable) slang, and racial name-calling. I could get in just as much trouble in my house for using the N-word as I could for using the F-word. Why is that? For one thing, both were just "ugly" words—words my grandfather would have called "vulgar"—words that only "common" people used. Both those words made you sound like you regularly mixed with the wrong sort of folks—something Christians were explicitly discouraged from doing.

The other reason I think we weren't permitted to use "language"—as in, "What kind of *language* is that for a *Christian* to use?"—was because it was thought to stain something profoundly within us, something that threatened "our relationship with Christ." We didn't say that kind of thing because, of course, it wounded the people about whom we were speaking (which is against the cardinal rule that covers being unfailingly nice), but more importantly because it put your relationship with Christ at risk, and that had eternal implications.

But here's the thing: Though I was discouraged from using racially offensive language on a personal level, I never made the connection with a larger system of racial injustice that produced people capable of speaking about other human beings in that way. I never learned that just refraining from using the N-word was only the beginning of Christian responsibility to other people whom God created.

On balance, I grew up feeling justified when it came to the issue of racism. I never owned slaves. Nobody I knew ever owned slaves. It never occurred to me that evaluating somebody on the basis of race for a job or a friendship or a lover was ever acceptable. I didn't use the N-word. What else could possibly be expected of me?

Activists weren't my people. My people didn't march; we didn't agitate; we didn't "sit in"; we didn't advocate. Not that my people considered those things necessarily wrong—or even that it would have been actively frowned upon. It's just that I never made the connection between my responsibilities to the world I lived in and what I thought it meant to follow Jesus—apart from what it might mean for my personal salvation.

The Problem I Think Many Young People Have with the Church

The whole personal relationship thing kept me going through childhood and adolescence; it seems perfectly suited to adolescence, which occupies much of its waking time with questions about personal relationships. That is to say, I take it that the whole point of adolescence is to help us see how the rest of the world relates to us.

Growing up, on the other hand, dramatically shifts the focus to the ways *we* are related to the rest of the world. I know that's a fine distinction linguistically. In practice, though, it makes all the difference in the world.

In beginning to understand the worth of things, if the center of gravity is me, then everything has a relative value only in relationship to me. You become more or less important depending on what part you play in my personal psychodrama. This seems to me to describe my practical understanding of things when I was a teenager. However, as I've grown up (or perhaps that's what growing up really is), I've begun to see that people and things have a value independent of their relationship to me. You have your own projects and dreams that are just as important to you as mine are to me. You aren't, in other words, a bit player, or worse, a handy prop in the "Theater of Derek."

"Please get to the point."

Ok. The kind of faith that shaped me as a young Evangelical tended toward abstraction.

"What? What does that even mean?"

How about this? It rarely occurred to me that my responsibility for the world and its inhabitants extended much beyond how my personal salvation might be affected.

"Wow! That seems pretty cold. I know plenty of Evangelicals who are warm, and who genuinely care about others and the world they inhabit. Don't you think that's kind of an unfair characterization?"

It is certainly broad, I'll admit. I'm not necessarily indicting all of Evangelicalism as self-absorbed soteriological narcissists. What I am saying, however, is that that was *my* experience of it. And perhaps more importantly, because it's an easy stereotype, it's the view many young people have of Evangelicals. Whether this stereotype of Evangelicalism is an accurate portrayal of Evangelical beliefs is open to question. However, because this stereotype of Evangelicalism is so widespread, and because popular culture often conflates Evangelicalism and Christianity, mainline Christians feel it necessary to expend a great deal of energy assuring everyone that "Yes, I am a Christian, but no, I'm not one of *those* kinds of Christian."

In my work with Millennials and Gen-Xers, among those who've dropped out of church, I regularly run into the assumption that Christianity is primarily about saving your own spiritual bacon. Here's what many young people think of Christians:

Screw the planet! Screw everyone else! As long as I get my own heavenly bus pass stamped, I've done what Jesus asked me to do.

Now, whether that's a fair characterization is another argument. That it is common, however, means the church, if it is to have any hope of connecting with these young people, is going to have to address it. "It," in this case, is what I call "The Jesus Gap."

The Jesus Gap

"If you follow Jesus and don't end up dead, it appears you have some explaining to do."

—TERRY EAGLETON[1]

There's a gap. I'm convinced of it. A Jesus gap.

There's a growing dissatisfaction with the traditional view of the church among emerging generations. This dissatisfaction has any number of causes, which the disaffected would name as anti-institutionalism, hypocrisy, judgmentalism, etc. But there's one area of vexation that always seems to come up: the Jesus Gap.

People, especially young people, are having trouble squaring the Jesus they read about in the Gospels with the infinitely malleable Jesus they see placed on offer by popular Christianity: Jesus as personal genie, Jesus as chief security guard at the courthouse of private morality, Jesus as a cheerleader for free-market capitalism, etc. In my work with emerging generations, we often return to the same complaint: "The Jesus I *read* about in church doesn't look like the Jesus I *see* in church." Whether it's Jesus as either a clearinghouse for heavenly bus passes or Jesus as Affirmer-in-Chief whose primary function revolves around endorsing middle-class American values, the Jesus of the Gospels fails to come through. This Jesus, when stripped of the layers of religious spackling used to domesticate him, is irremediably subversive.

Subversive. That appeals to me. Of course, I'd like to continue writing clinically about the religious climate shift underway at the hands of restless "young people" fed up with a tame Jesus. I'd like to make it sound as though I'm just a disinterested observer of religious trends. But the truth is that I too find myself growing dissatisfied with that tame and restricted image of Jesus. After all these years of a Jesus who I thought would help make me _____ (holier? kinder? more spiritual? more self-actualized?), I've come to believe that Jesus has a more cosmic, more interesting agenda in mind than super-tuning my soul. On my way to spiritual superstardom, I've found it increasingly difficult to squeeze past the Gospels' Jesus, who

---

[1]Terry Eagleton, *Reason, Faith, and Revolution: Reflections on the God Debate,* The Terry Series (New Haven, Conn.. Yale Univesity Press, 2009).

stands in the middle of the road pointing to the weak, the homeless, the sick, the widowed, the displaced and unembraced. Following Jesus; I think it boils down to that, really.

I've struggled for some time with the realization that when the church fails—as it often does—it fails most egregiously in giving people the resources necessary for the outrageously radical act of following Jesus. My reading of Emerging/ent theology has led me to conclude that there is increasing energy around the simple idea that followers of Jesus ought to embody the revolutionary spirit found in the Gospels.

I've tried. I've put forth a valiant effort. But I can no longer envision Jesus the way I once did. I can't, for the life of me, picture Jesus saying, "Healthcare isn't a right; it's a privilege."

I can't figure out a way to get Jesus to say, "Homosexuality is a capital crime, but fleecing the poor is a misdemeanor."

I can't imagine a world in which Jesus says, "If you don't let children pray to me in school, I'll let armed gunmen come in and kill them indiscriminately."

I'm trying to track down, but as of yet have been unable to find, where Jesus says, "If you fear someone will strike you on one cheek, dial in a Predator drone."

The church has too often been asked to give religious cover to moralities that were conceived absent the theological reflection provided by the church. I find that the chasm between the revolutionary Jesus of first century Jerusalem and the domesticated Jesus of twenty-first century America grows more difficult for me to span all the time.

In the final analysis, the good news of the reign of God is not first that the well taken care of will be even more well taken care of in the *next* life. The good news of the reign of God is that God's reign is present wherever the homeless are sheltered, wherever the hungry are fed, wherever the rich give away their money and power in defense of the poor, wherever the forgotten ones gather to be remembered and embraced, to be told that as long as we follow God, not one of God's children will be left to die alone and unloved.

Why Are Millennials Leaving the Church?

The church where I serve made a decision last year to support its ministers in refusing to sign marriage licenses until the rights of marriage could be conferred upon LGTBQ couples. The decision brought national attention, the overwhelming majority of which was positive.

One group in particular who responded to the decision surprised me. I never saw it coming. Some of the most gratifying reactions came from the adult children of some of the older members of our congregation, which is to say, from young people who had dropped out of church a long time ago. From across the U.S. I got word from these displaced folks. They emailed, called, messaged me through social media, and, the ones who still live close by, buttonholed me on the street. Their comments shared one thing in common: "I'm so proud to tell my friends that the church that did this cool thing is the church I grew up in."

Then, a couple of them proceeded to say something that was hard to hear: "I never thought I'd see a church do something so Christian." Embedded in that response is something worth hearing about the way an increasing number of young people experience the church. According to a recent article on Sojourners Blog, Millennials are headed for the exits, even among Evangelicals.[2] Why? According to the article, which cites research by the Barna Group, "Research indicates younger people are not only departing from their elders on 'social issues,' such as same-sex marriage and abortion, but on wealth distribution and care for the environment, as well" (http://www.barna.org/store?page=shop.product_details&flypage=flypage.tpl&product_id=128).

One way to look at the difference Millennials represent on these kinds of social issues is that they've been seduced by an increasingly secular society. From the time they were young, this thinking goes, the culture has offered Millennials a vision of human life that is often at odds with the vision claimed by churches, one focused less and less on God. Politically, "liberals" have successfully appealed to youthful passion and idealism, rendering them dewey-eyed woolgatherers who know little either about God or about how the world "really" works. As a consequence, Millennials come to their convictions about the purpose of human life and its just embodiment either as a result of theological ignorance or theological rebellion. The implication is that if they *really* new about Christianity, they wouldn't believe such outrageous things about marriage, economic equality, and environmental responsibility.

There are a couple of different responses that come to mind, if this is the way you frame the problem of the disappearance of young adults. On the one hand, you could just tell young people they're wrong, and they need

---

[2]From   http://sojo.net/blogs/2011/12/20/millennials-church-wake-or-were-outta-here?page=show. I think the same might be said, if perhaps to a lesser extent of Gen X-ers. But I'll respond only to the claims about Millennials, since they are the focus of the article.

to get right. In many cases, this was the strategy employed by the Greatest Generation when Baby Boomers started questioning organized religion in the 1960s and '70s. For those who think this kind of "unvarnished truth" strategy is the way to go, it might be helpful to contemplate its success when used on an earlier generation—take a look at *The Big Chill*, for instance.

On the other hand, you might look at the exodus of Millennials as a failure of relevance. Churches got sidetracked, started focusing on stuff Millennials found pointless—stuff like bigger buildings, keeping up social appearances for the country club set, right wing politics, etc. If you interpret irrelevance to be the reason young people don't want anything to do with the church, you have an easy way to address the issue: Be more relevant. Find cool-looking people to play cool-sounding music. Say "dude" a lot. Make sure you know the difference between a cappuccino and a latte. Easy.

There are a couple of different branches of über relevance available, too. If you're sympathetic to the whole mega-church movement, sprinkle some Jesus over the top of ordinary stuff young people like, and voilà, instant relevance. Christian rock climbing. Christian aerobics. Christian skateboarding. Christian Screamo bands. The possibilities are endless.

If you find an emergent emphasis more to your liking, you'll need another set of accouterments. Tattoos are good. Piercings and ear gauges add a nice touch. Make sure to do some outings in a pub, with lots of locally microbrewed fare. Relevance isn't too far off.

And while I happen to think the emergent movement is much more theologically interesting for a whole host of reasons other than just those things that accessorize it, like the mega-church stuff, if it's just a marketing strategy for obtaining relevance, I think it's doomed to drive Millennials away. Millennials have been socialized to be amazingly aware of being marketed to, and they react poorly to such poses adopted solely for the purpose of "winning" their spiritual "business."

I find all of these ways of reading the departure of young adults from the church dismissive, sharing a common misconception that what's wrong, what's driving Millennials away from the church, resides somewhere *outside* the church (either with Millennials themselves or with the culture that produced them)—or that if it is the church's fault, the problems are merely cosmetic, easily remedied by superficial tweaks here or there.

There's another way of reading the generational tea leaves, however, one that places responsibility on the church, not for failing to be relevant, but for failing to be faithful to the Jesus found in the Gospels. Maybe the problem is that Millennials hear about Jesus and then take him at his word. Maybe they really believe that stuff Jesus says at the beginning of his ministry in Luke: "The Spirit of the Lord is upon me, because he has anointed me to bring good news to the poor. He has sent me to proclaim release to the captives and recovery of sight to the blind, to let the oppressed go free, to proclaim the year of the Lord's favor" (4:18-19).

Then, they go to church, and instead of hearing about how to live with those who've been kicked to the curb, how to be Christ to a world caving in on itself, they hear about how the church's job is to maneuver itself into positions of power, respectability, relevance, and so on.

They hear about committee meetings and deficit budgets and why it is imperative that we "keep Christ in Christmas."

They hear a baptized politics that exhorts them to be good moral "individuals" who seek a "personal relationship with Jesus," but their relationship to the poor and the powerless, their relationship to an economic system designed to serve the interests of those already on top at the expense of those on the bottom, their relationship to a government that starts preemptive wars based on a conceit, their relationship to God's creation—these are largely matters of indifference to the church.

These young people go to church and hear why (if they happen to be at a conservative church) gay people are going to hell, or (if they happen to be at a more "progressive" church) why it might upset the ecclesiastical apple cart if we were to say that gay people are created in the image of God—exactly the way God wanted them.

All of which is to say: Maybe it's not Millennials who've left the church so much as that the church has left Jesus—and Millennials are the only ones brave enough to recognize that the emperor has been parading about without the benefit of clothes. If that's the case, the church would do well to quit worrying so much about whether Millennials are leaving the church, and start investing time and effort and resources into looking more like Jesus. Then Millennials might finally see something for which it would be worth sticking around.

"I'm so proud to tell my friends that the church that did this cool thing is the church I grew up in" isn't the same as "How do I sign up to get back into church?" For any number of really important reasons, though, it's a step in the right direction.

"Tell me what you want, not what you want to avoid."

"What do you want to do when you get out of college?" That was the question on the table.

Summer camp. We were gathered together with one of the grizzled veteran counselors to talk about what we planned to do with our lives. Having just graduated from high school, we found the whole conversation a bit abstract. We didn't know what we were going to do with our lives. And we certainly didn't want to be reminded about the fact that we didn't know. But somebody asked the question, and we were all raised with the kind of manners that wouldn't allow us to say what we were thinking: "I really don't want to think about this. Ask me about the beach or about what we're going to do when we *get* to college. After college is just too far away."

One girl said, "Well, I don't want to have to do a job I hate, where I'm stuck doing the same thing over and over—like a factory. And I don't want to work someplace that makes me do busy work just to satisfy some kind of Human Resources directive intended to create a 'positive working environment.'"

"Ok. What kind of working environment do you *want* to work in?"

"I don't want work with a lot of passive-aggressive people—you know, the kind who get mad about little things and start putting up signs about not eating their yogurt or taking the stapler off their desk."

"You run into a lot of sign hangers, a lot of yogurt and stapler thieves in high school, did you?"

"No, but I hear my dad talk about it all the time."

"Anyone else?"

A longhaired guy in a denim jacket and boots said, "I don't want to have do any job that requires me to wear a name tag or be a part of a 'team'" (his use of air quotes, tipping us off to his studied use of sarcasm).

I jumped in and said, "Look, I just don't want to have to get up too early in the morning." I was not particularly ambitious.

The counselor, showing signs of frustration, said, "You've obviously thought about this. Here's what I want, though. Tell me what you want to *do*, not what you want to *avoid* doing. What are your dreams? What makes you excited enough to get out of bed in the morning—regardless of the time?

What do you care about so much you'd be willing to die for?"

As cliché as it may sound, more people in emerging generations know Christianity by what it stands against than by what it stands for. Jesus, though he clearly had strong opinions about what people should stay away from, seemed on balance more concerned about the kind of things in which people should be investing their lives.

This full-throated commitment to *doing* something got Jesus in trouble. In Matthew, he is contrasted with the ascetic John the Baptist: "For John came neither eating nor drinking, and they say, 'He has a demon;' the Son of Man came eating and drinking, and they say, 'Look, a glutton and a drunkard, a friend of tax-collectors and sinners!'" (11:18-19). It's important to point out that Jesus drew the contrast between himself and John the Baptist to indicate that there's just no pleasing some people, no matter what you do. However, it is also worth noting that Jesus developed a reputation, not for the things he avoided, but for the things he threw himself into.

In a post-denominational world, the church must be aware of the widely held perception that it cares more about *keeping* people from doing things than about giving them the resources they need to follow Jesus. As commitment to mainline denominations deteriorates, the church would do well to think more intentionally about how it embodies its vision of the reign of God. Justice. Equity. Mutuality. Community. Compassion for the poor, the outcast, the powerless. These are positive visions.

"But isn't that just a rehash of the traditional liberalism mainline denominations have been trying to interest people in since the latter part of the nineteenth century? If it were such a winning strategy, why are mainline denominations dying?"

Excellent point! I realize I'm trying to thread a pretty fine needle here. What I'm suggesting, though, isn't a *strategy* (I don't think traditional liberal mainliners necessarily thought the Social Gospel was just a strategy either). Making strategic decisions about justice in God's reign as a way to attract more people misses the whole point. Justice, equity, mutuality, and the like are what we think Jesus came to establish. He did not come to give us well-devised membership recruitment tools.

In a post-denominational world, the church needs to quit thinking first about how to save its own bacon, and start devoting more thought to doing the right thing—because we have no other way of conceiving our lives as followers of Jesus.

Aristotle and the Reason Why Churches So Often Get It Wrong

Aristotle said that there are two kinds of moral action—those acts that are *intrinsically good* (i.e., "good in themselves") and those acts that are *instrumentally good*. [3]

"Oh crap, here he goes again."

Just hang with me a minute. An act is intrinsically good if it can't be said to be done for any reason external to it. An act is instrumentally good if it can be said to be done in the service of something else.

"Kill me, please."

No, wait. All right. I tell my kids to do their homework. So, they do their homework. Why?

"Because you told them to do it."

And they might do it because they want to please me, or because they fear displeasing me.

"Exactly."

Are there any other reasons why they might do their homework, totally unrelated to me?

"They might do their homework because they want to succeed and go to college, or perhaps because they don't want to fail and risk not being able to go to college."

True enough. Any other reason?

"They like it?"

Exactly! Maybe they do it because it brings them pleasure. Maybe they do it because the work itself is satisfying, because it offers them the chance not only to practice and learn, but because the practice and learning offer something good they can't find anywhere else but in the work itself. [4]

Steven Pressfield notes one of the central truths of the Bhagavad Gita: "The laborer is entitled only to her labor, not to its fruits" (Pressfield, 88). In other words, what you do should be its own reward. You have to learn to love what you do for its own sake, not for what it can bring you in the

---

[3]This is going to be grossly simplified, so don't email me.

[4]I will concede that this may very well be only a theoretical, if not a practical, option.

way of reward or applause (or in the church's case—young families, a bigger operating budget, inflated membership roles, etc.).

Please understand, I'm not saying that the fruit of your labor is necessarily bad. I'm just saying that seeking first the fruit makes your labor only *instrumentally* good. That is to say, you do what you do—homework, your job, macrame, or ministry—only because you get something in exchange for it, something out of it. It's far better for you to do what you've been called to do whether or not you ever realize any benefit from it.

"Why?"

Because you need to spend your time, your resources, your passion, your life on something, the value of which is *intrinsic* to it. A sad reality of Capitalism is that one of the things it teaches us is to determine the value of a thing instrumentally—by what it's worth on the open market. (This is one of the reasons why science and math, for instance, often suck all the oxygen out of the academic atmosphere. Humanities—art, literature, music, philosophy, religion—are notoriously difficult to monetize.)

What Do *We* Get Out of It?

So, here's the thing: Churches have a bad habit of asking this question first.

The answer to the question, "Why should we invest in this ministry?" if it is to be *intrinsically* and not *instrumentally* good is: "Because it's the right thing to do." Regardless of whether we ever realize any benefit from the costly investments of time and resources required by ministry, we do what we do because God wants it done. We take pleasure in the labor, not in its fruits. Cost-benefit analysis, whether it's a good way to assess the value of investing in Facebook stock, isn't necessarily the best way to appraise the value of a soup kitchen, or a latchkey program, or an AIDS ministry.

Viewed from the perspective of Rome (and some of the Jewish leaders—at least according to the Gospels), Jesus' execution was viewed as an acceptable price to pay—to the Romans for heading off what they assumed was a possible revolutionary, and to the Jewish leaders whose authority Jesus' ministry often called into question. In other words, from the perspective of Jesus' opponents, his execution was viewed as an instrumental good in the service of larger goals.

Emerging generations in a post-denominational world are acutely aware of a sales job. What they value are things like authenticity, transparency, genuine commitment. Whether mainline churches "survive" is largely beside the point. Many people outside the church would love to see things unravel, since they think the church is responsible for much of what's wrong with the world. A large percentage of people outside the church don't care one way or another about its survival. And those outsiders, who would like to see it survive, care more about the church's usefulness in creating a slightly more civil society.

I'm arguing that if the mainline denominations have any chance of doing something important and interesting (read faithful), they will begin to think more about the positive vision of God's reign that they want to embody than the negative vision of what they want to avoid—whether what they want to avoid is bad behavior or their own demise. They will begin to think more in terms of the reign of God present in the world rather than in the celestial sales job of convincing people what's wrong with their lives is that they don't have Jesus comfortably housed in their hearts. They will begin to leave behind a preoccupation with the self—whether individual or corporate—and launch out into the world with revolutionary and reckless abandon.

To get an idea of what I'm envisioning for churches in a post-denominational world, it might be easier to look at it through the lens of the Buddha's Four Noble Truths.

Letting Go

In the Deer Park Discourses, the Buddha famously observed that "life is suffering"—the first noble truth—which, when first heard by students in my world religion classes, strikes them as unnecessarily morose.

"Yeah, life sucks and all that ... but it's not all bad."

At that point, I explain to them that the word used by the Buddha (*dukkha*), which often gets translated from the Pali as "suffering," doesn't just mean something like "unremitting agony." It can mean that, of course; but it means much more. *Dukkha* is better understood as a wheel in which the axle is off center, making the wheel wobble constantly as it turns. *Dukkha* is like a pebble in the shoe, which can cause great pain, but is more often experienced as a phenomenon that exists just beneath the horizon of awareness, always seeming to lurk at the edges of consciousness. It is, in short, the nagging sense that something is not right. Suffering then is not in the epic sense of the grand heroic struggle, but in the dislocative sense that life is not as it should be.

Why is life *dukkha*? According to the Buddha, the second noble truth is that life is *dukkha* because we desire.

"Of course, we desire. Why is that bad?"

Again, I stop to explain that the word the Buddha used (*tanha*) is probably better translated "selfishly grasp." We suffer because we grasp after things intended only to satisfy ourselves. We want things because *we* want them, and when we don't get them, we experience suffering.

Our selfish grasping causes us to treat things as permanent, which things are only transitory (*anicca*). I believe that this time love will last forever; that my new _____ (fill in the blank) won't break, rust, expire, or wear out; that the body that has served me so well in the past will persist through time. When that which we grasp for inevitably stops working, leaves, runs dry, we suffer.

Moreover, as the Buddha observed, we're extremely proficient at lying to ourselves about the nature of our existence (*anatta*). We tell ourselves that the world we inhabit is the real world and not just the world we perceive, that truth is an easy thing to possess for ourselves and not for our enemies, that we are who we believe ourselves to be. When we find out the extent to which we cling to illusions, we suffer.

By now, my students are itching to argue with the Buddha. That's when I break out the third noble truth. The third noble truth consists in seeing the first two noble truths together as inextricably bound up with one another, then seeking to untangle them. The Buddha said, "If you want not to suffer, you must not selfishly grasp."

"That's fine for the Buddha; he gave everything away. He didn't have anything left to hold onto."

Exactly!

Jesus said something very much like this about 500 years later: "For those who want to save their life will lose it, and those who lose their life for my sake, and for the sake of the gospel, will save it. For what will it profit them to gain the whole world and forfeit their life?" (Mark 8:35–36).

So, here's the thing. Congregations and Denominations are not unlike individuals in their mad scramble to hold onto something, to grasp after that which is impermanent.

Have you ever been to a church where desperation hangs in the air—the feeling that "we've got to do something, or we're going to die?"

Have you ever been to a denominational meeting where executives are in a mad scramble to preserve their own "indispensable" department?

Have you ever been to a church where every meeting is punctuated by hand-wringing over money? The lack of young families? Declining worship attendance?

Have you ever been to a church where everything centers on making sure I get *my* heavenly bus pass stamped?

Have you ever been to a church where failure is not viewed as a learning experience, but as one more step down the inevitable path toward extinction?

Dukkha. Tanha. According to Jesus and the Buddha, they're causally related. The more you have of the latter, the more you can be sure you have of the former.

If you want not to suffer, you must relinquish your grasping. That is to say, you must disentangle yourself from that which causes your suffering. You must detach from those things, ideas, expectations to which you cling so desperately. Turn loose.

"Again, easy for you to say."

But it's not easy for me to say, and it's even harder for me to do. I didn't say it was easy, only necessary. Jesus says the cost of the whole process is a cross, which is to say, death (Mk 8:34). That's why titling this book "A Mainliner's Survival Guide to the Post-Denominational World" is misleading. If you think the ordinary meaning of surviving means "hanging on a little bit tighter for a little bit longer," this book is going to be an enormous disappointment. "Survival," at least in the paradoxical sense Jesus envisions, means letting go, turning loose, laying down, dying—dying to the idea that you've got anything worth hanging onto that God doesn't already own.

Field Notes

So, maybe the way to think about it looks something like this:

- Have you ever been to a church where the big appeal is to what you can give away, what you can sacrifice, what you can lay down, instead of on what you can gain, what you can grasp, what you can hold to your breast?

- Have you ever been to a church that spends more time struggling over what to give away than what to keep—that is, it expends more energy on the Outreach committee than on the Property committee?

- Have you ever been to a church that sees its small youth group not as a disappointment but as an opportunity to offer more focused ministry?

- Have you ever been to a church that views its building as a present to the world and not as a bequest to its members?

- Have you ever been to a church where worship is centered on the gift that is offered to God rather than on what individual participants "get out of it?"

- Have you ever been to a church where truth is a friend and illusion is the thing to be avoided at all cost?

- Have you ever been to a church in which justice is not just the securing of individual rights but the pursuit of a vision of the reign of God in which there is no justice until it gets extended to everyone?

I wish there were handy "practical tips" I could give you on how to tweak a few things when it comes to this stuff. Unfortunately, there aren't any shortcuts. This takes a radical reorientation to the world in which we find ourselves. This, it seems to me, is what real conversion looks like (impending doom close notwithstanding).

In a post-denominational world, the way forward seems clear: The church must be more concerned with relinquishing any idea of success that doesn't begin with death, sacrifice, laying down. The church must focus on letting go of the need to ensure its future rather than on grasping for its survival. Letting go means giving up everything, perhaps even the life to which we cling so desperately.

Take heart, though: if you follow Jesus, you already have a pretty good idea what giving it all away looks like.

8

"Are We Meeting at the Coffee House or the Pub?" or the Church as Radical Community

Aunt B's

Two weeks after graduating from college, I got married. We were young. We moved to Tennessee so I could go to seminary, which, because I couldn't find work, proved to be a short stay. Feeling like a failure in life at twenty-two, my young bride and I moved back to Detroit to live with my in-laws.

Eventually I found work. And after a hard-charging year as an assistant manager at the local Speedway and as a press operator, stamping out clutch plates at a tool and die shop, we decided to brave the wilds of Tennessee again. I moved down a month ahead of my wife, couch surfing with a couple of friends from college and delivering pizzas for Domino's. When I finally found a job as a youth minister at a country church, I felt like our prospects for making a go of it had improved considerably.

We found an apartment. I started classes. And things, though a bit shaky, seemed headed in the right direction. Unfortunately, after a few months, we found that we couldn't afford the apartment. So in January we moved to a little three room post-war house in the country with a tin roof, heated by a coal stove in the living room. Rent—$150 a month. We called it the "Love Shack."

The reason I give all that seemingly pointless detail is to set the context for my state of mind at the time. As a young northerner, transplanted from Detroit to Tennessee, I found myself cut off from some extremely important support systems. Following the dream of post-secondary education, I left behind—what felt like to me—everything I knew. Family and friends were twelve hours away. Culturally, I felt like a Connecticut Yankee in Cold Mountain. When I tried to catch the baseball scores on the six o'clock local news, the broadcasts led with lake levels for the bass fishing report.

Isolated. Disoriented. Depressed. Apart from my wife and my work, I felt lost.

At the end of my first year, however, we made some friends from the seminary. Our new friends were transplants also. We fell into one another's arms like people reuniting on the deck of the Coast Guard rescue ship after being plucked out of raging black seas. We spent every spare moment together, clinging to one another lest we find ourselves once again battling the waves.

My new friends and I started gathering at a little greasy spoon a half mile up the road called Aunt B's. It sat off the main road, tucked in next to the auto repair shop. It was an elegant arrangement: the husband ran the garage, and the wife served up diner fare. Over time I noticed a great deal of cross-pollination between the two establishments. Come get your transmission worked on and have some meatloaf while you wait. Aunt B's was the kind of place where you got your own coffee, where the tables all had sugar packets or folded up napkins under one leg, and where Ethel, the head waitress, knew what you wanted—only coming to the table to make sure you hadn't changed your mind and gotten adventurous, thinking you'd try some new starch-based entrée.

As seminarians we were supposed to go to chapel a few times a week. Instead, we generally headed out to Aunt B's. We drank coffee, smoked cigarettes, read the paper, and talked. We talked a lot. We talked about sports and theology, about our families and our jobs, about where we were on our theses and what we were going to do after we had to leave and go start real lives. Notwithstanding the seminary administration's opinion to the contrary, we considered it our own version of chapel.

In fact, for two years Aunt B's helped put an anchor in the roiling waters of my uncertain life. And over time, though our group is spread out all over the country, most of us have held hands through divorces, remarriages, babies, changing jobs, and the illness and death of our parents.

Aunt B's struck me at the time (and in many ways strikes me still) as what I thought the church ought to be—a place where people can go to find companions and fellow travelers, to find support and accountability, to find meaning, purpose, and sometimes just a reason to hang on. Aunt B's became for me a kind of archetype of community in which it is possible to find God in the faces of people who know you and love you amid the quotidian phenomena of clanging pans and cigarette smoke.

I realize now that I've spent most of my adult life and ministry trying to find the kind of community I felt at Aunt B's—sometimes successfully, most times in vain. And while I understand that there exists in my search a certain gilded nostalgia for a time and place that had its own share of too easily forgotten problems, that experience of community at one point helped save the church for me, and it continues to help me sustain a vision of what the embodied reign of God might look like.

Needing a Place to Belong

We live in the most mobile and often the most disconnected culture in the history of the world. Young people are told from an early age that success in life requires a college education. After graduating from college, often with a mountain of student loan debt, young people find themselves in the awkward position of having to find jobs, less according to vocational and personal compatibility or prospects for advancement or even for geographic proximity to family and friends than for whether a job will pay them enough to pay back the bank. Consequently, with few exceptions, we've created a society that requires the possibility of mobility as the price of admission. Follow the money.

"It says here that you are exceptionally well qualified for this position. If we offer you the job, are you prepared to move to our Schenectady branch?"

"Do you have anything in the Midwest? I'd kind of like to stay closer to my family."

"Next."

Of course, mobility isn't just a problem for young people. Owing to the vagaries of a turbulent economy, even people long established in a career are having to uproot to pursue employment.

Moreover, with advances in healthcare leading to an increase in life span, older people find themselves more and more in the unenviable position of having to make a decision to pack up their settled lives, leaving friends and established commitments, to go where their adult children are. Multi-generational families are becoming increasingly common, which often comes with the ironic effect of costing seniors by limiting their participation in non-familial communities of friends and volunteer commitments.[1]

The kinds of ties that have traditionally rooted people geographically are being severed at alarming rates. Of course, great migrations in search of new ways of making a living have occurred in history before. But apart from strictly nomadic cultures, those who took off in search of new land, new opportunities, new worlds intended to put down fresh roots and form permanent communities when they arrived at their destinations. People in this mobile society don't necessarily have those goals, especially young people.

After the Revolutionary War, for instance, a segment of the population became pioneers in search of new lives on the frontier and headed westward. These travelers were usually accompanied by a band of people committed to the same objective, all of whom were leaving behind the comfort and security of established communities. This westward expansion cost those adventurous souls a great deal, not least their sense of belonging. However, the goal of these treks to the borders of civilization was to find a place to put down new roots. In fact, the brave souls who made the journey were often referred to as "settlers."

In today's mobile society people also explore new frontiers in search of starting a new life. However, the primary goal of today's pilgrims often has less to do with putting down new roots than with taking strategic steps on a career path headed somewhere else, or with staying one step ahead of the bill collector, or with avoiding the nursing home. And because of shifting economic conditions, today's pioneers have less the air of "settler" about them than of itinerants in search of the next thing.

In leaving behind communities, however, people don't abandon that innate need to belong. Aristotle knew this, famously calling human beings "political animals." He believed that humans had a function, an ultimate purpose for being. This purpose for being is both discovered and shaped by belonging to a *polis*—a community of people, bound together by a need to belong to something larger. So great was this need to belong, Aristotle said that any person who did not have need of a *polis* was either a beast or a god.

---

[1] See, for instance, Atieno Oduor, et al. "Grandparents Caring for their Grandchildren: Emerging Roles and Exchanges in Global Perspectives." *Journal Of Comparative Family Studies* 40, no. 5 (September 2009): 827–848.

People, no matter how modern or sophisticated, need to belong, to have some place where they can find and cultivate friendships. The mobility of our contemporary society doesn't forestall this need. In fact, I would suggest that our penchant for rootlessness underscores the intensity of our need for making friends.

I spoke with a young man not long ago, just recently graduated from college. He'd moved away from a small town to a big city to go to a state university in a major metropolitan area. He loves the city, and has no desire to go back to his hometown. He has a pretty good job, but he doesn't know how long it will last. His friends who've graduated from college with him are busy with new jobs or, just as likely, *looking* for new jobs. His longtime girlfriend just graduated and is pursuing various job prospects as a teacher. Unfortunately, some of the best offers she's received have come from places in different parts of the state, requiring them both to make big decisions.

Lately, he's become aware of the disruption in his life. There are no structural components in his schedule that require his presence in situations with people he wants to be with—no classes, no intramurals, no dorm life, no casual contact achieved by bumping into a friend in the cafeteria or the student union. If he wants to get together with his friends, he has to make a conscious decision to call or text, check calendars against work and personal commitments, and then set up a time.

In other words, my young friend is discovering the cliché that most adults know and routinely comment on: The older you get, the more difficult it is to make friends. Outside of work, most adults have to decide to put themselves in situations where friendship is possible. For many in our highly mobile culture, childhood friends, high school friends, college friends all seem to have moved on, following an uncertain job market wherever it leads.

How do you make friends? Where do you go to belong to something that promises to fulfill the longing for community?

The Church as Polis

A generation ago William Willimon and Stanley Hauerwas wrote *Resident Aliens: The Church as Polis*, a book challenging Christians to understand themselves, not as formed by their participation in the broader culture, but as members of a Christian outpost in a strange land, formed by their commitments to following Christ. The book proved controversial. Many of its critics charged that Willimon and Hauerwas were arguing for a kind of tribalism that called Christians to retreat from engagement with the world.

Others saw it as permission to stop following the relentless admonition to "be relevant."

As a young minister, having grown up in an Evangelical subculture that desperately sought to prove its relevance, I found the book liberating. It spoke to my sense that Christianity was about something much more than what it appeared to me to be, an attempt to baptize popular culture by slapping Jesus stickers on everything. I had grown weary of the indiscriminate use of "Christian" as an adjective. In an attempt to prove Jesus could make anything better, popular Christianity introduced such unfortunate diversions as "Christian aerobics" and "Christian theme parks." A very lucrative industry emerged, selling Christian T-shirts, bumper stickers, and wall hangings. You could listen to Christian rock-and-roll, surrounded by people wearing Christian jewelry, sporting Christian neckties, and sucking on Christian breath mints. The idea appeared to be that whatever "the world" did, Christians could improve on it simply by adding a cross or a Jesus fish.

The creation of a popular Christian sub-culture succeeded in making a lot of people a boatload of money, but only succeeded in portraying Christians to outsiders—the very ones who were supposed to be impressed by the relevance—as wannabes.

"See? Jesus can be cool too!"

I eventually found this unctuousness embarrassing—like when your dad goes through a mid-life crisis and starts trying too hard to prove that he can still "hang with the kids" but never sounds quite right saying things like "dude." Willimon and Hauerwas pointed toward a path that allowed Christians to take their faith seriously, without having to preoccupy themselves with whether or not the world applauds. I found their argument challenging, completely lacking the perpetual sense of approval seeking.

Part of what they set down in the book centers on a move away from the radical individualism of the Enlightenment. The Enlightenment, in offering up reason as the opponent to revelation, dramatically shifted the seat of authority. Prior to the Enlightenment, authority for identifying what knowledge even *is* resided in the hands of a group—the *polis* or the church. But with the advent of Renè Descartes' famous epistemological examination of what one can know with certainty, *who* gets to say what qualifies as knowledge moves from the community represented by the church to the individual.

"Ok, smarty-pants, slow down."

Let me try it this way. Before the Enlightenment, some *group* always had the final say about what was true, what could be considered a "fact." As a result of the Enlightenment, individuals get to decide for themselves what's true and what to consider fact.

"Like what?"

Scientists have said for years that the world we inhabit exists as the result of billions of years of adaptations, called "evolution." These scientists argue that the weight of the evidence surrounding evolution overwhelmingly prompts us to say that this hypothesis should be considered true. Certain segments of the religious population, on the other hand, wanting to remain faithful to what they believe to be the biblical truth presented in the story of a literal six-day creation, look at the claims put forward by scientists and say: "We don't like your version of the 'truth' about how we got here. And we reserve the right to choose our own version of it." (Hint: The scare quotes are the tip-off.)

Individual choice emerges as one of the most important characteristics of modernity—that post-Enlightenment period characterized by "the turn to the self," in which truth has less to do with something "out there" than with my right to choose whom to trust as an authority about what's "out there." The argument about evolution, for example, is not about whether the facts of science or the facts of the Bible are more reliable, but about whether science or the Bible has the right to claim legitimating authority for what's true. In other words, after the Enlightenment some group doesn't declare and impose truth on individuals. Instead, individuals choose what group is in a position to know what's true. Authority has shifted from the many to the one.

"So what?"

Apart from the implications for what it means to know things in the world we've inherited, it also pushed the individual back onto herself. Community, and the authority it had traditionally wielded, became a symbol of tyranny. Thomas Jefferson, not coincidentally, an important Enlightenment political theorist, sought to embed the principle of the individual in the very conception of the new government. In the *Declaration of Independence* he set down an important argument against the authority of any group to tell the individual how to live or what to value. According to Jefferson, it was the individual's right, and not some despotic community's, to choose how best to pursue such fundamentally important decisions as what constitutes the best and truest life, the liberty to choose it, and just what sorts of things lead to happiness as a result. In the Revolutionary Period, the seeds for the demise of community had been sown.

However, as Aristotle pointed out, we are political animals made for life together. This conflict between the turn to the self and the impulse toward belonging to some group exists profoundly among emerging generations. Christian Smith and Patricia Snell's work on emerging adults, *Souls in Transition*, concludes that there exists among Millennials and Generation Xers an uncomfortable paradox: they have a strong desire to become independent while at the same time clinging to the communal security of relationships with family and friends.

Let Me Do It Myself/Don't Leave Me Alone

When my wife and I moved back in with her parents, we felt like we had no other choice. Neither of us had jobs, the money from the wedding had long since disappeared, and bills began to mount. My wife, as has always been the case, found a job right away. In my own defense, it turns out having a bachelor's degree with a double major in New Testament and Language is much less lucrative than one might otherwise have reason to assume.

I found jobs rust-proofing cars and working for a new retail clothing chain, but those didn't last long. At twenty-two, I found myself with a college degree, a wife, affordable housing in my in-laws' basement, and no other way to support myself. I wallowed in depression. My young wife demonstrated much greater reserves of patience than I could have mustered in her position.

One day, I stopped to get gas at the corner Speedway where I noticed a sign that said they were hiring for an evening cashier. Any pride about asking for work had run screaming into the dark night of unemployed despair; so I filled out an application. The manager told me to come in the next night. I remember my ambivalence at the time. On the one hand, I desperately needed a job, even a job as a gas station cashier. On the other hand, I got a job as a *gas station cashier*, a job I initially felt entirely too good to do.

What proved interesting, though, was my wife's response. As soon as I had a steady gig, she grew increasingly unsatisfied living with her parents. Though she loved having the ties to her family, with whom she was very close, she felt that as newly minted grownups we had a responsibility to go out and start carving our own path. This compulsion to leave grew stronger with each passing day. Ironically, I took the other side of the debate, arguing that now that we were making money, living with her parents for awhile would allow us to save up. I said stay. She said go. So, we went.

We found an apartment four miles from her parents. Her dad came with us to cosign the lease. And we spent our first Christmas together in a little one bedroom apartment with a Christmas tree tied to the wall with sewing thread to make it stand up—since I didn't have the proper tools to straighten out the crooked trunk. Adults.

Emerging adults, as Smith and Snell have suggested, struggle with the issue of independence. They argue that "the central, fundamental, driving focus in life of nearly all emerging adults is getting themselves to the point where they can 'stand on their own two feet'" (Smith and Snell, 34).

Young people want to act like adults—make their own money, live in their own places, do the things they believe adults do. Unfortunately, the dream of independence is increasingly elusive, especially in light of the spiraling costs of education and the mounting pressure of student debt load. That they feel forced to defer "true" adulthood by continuing to live with their families causes frustration and feelings of inadequacy.

Desperately desiring independence, many young people find they must delay that important step on the way to maturity. But the desire to "stand on their own two feet" burns hot.

Paradoxically, the impulse to remain closely tied to those systems of emotional (and sometimes financial) support wars with the desire for independence. Wanting to maintain some kind of community that provides support, direction, and human connection lives within us all. However, young adults, because of the highly mobile nature of our society, are particularly aware of their need to stay connected.

This hunger for community, however, should not be confused with a hunger for "organization." Though young adults seek out social relationships, what they desire is the affinity and personal contact of those relationships, not necessarily the structure found in other kinds of public associations (Smith and Snell, 73). For those generations coming to maturity, seeking out groups whose primary cause for existing is to get something done is low down on the list of priorities.

What Does This Mean for Congregations in a Post-Denominational World?

If all I've been saying is true about the paradox of young adults who aspire to independence yet eagerly desire to maintain interpersonal relationships, congregations must recognize that young adults aren't looking to "join." They appear less interested in community-as-a-tool to accomplish some other purpose than community-as-an-opportunity to make and keep friends. This raises challenges for congregations in a post-denominational world seeking to provide a safe place where friendships can be made and community can develop among young adults.

On its face, this attachment to friendship for its own sake can cause alarm in older generations in the church who've traditionally understood church to work in almost the exact opposite way. In the past, denominations helped provide the kind of social stability I've been describing, a world in which friendships endured because people tended to stay in the same places. Denominational loyalty was a hallmark of this social stability. After becoming a part of a denomination, either through birth, conversion, or transfer of membership, people tended to identify with that denomination indefinitely. There was a time when it was common to hear someone self-describe as a "fourth generation Methodist," for example. Today, however, denominational loyalty appears to many as a quaint bit of nostalgia, like the gilded memories of neighborhood soda fountains and day baseball.

The religious stability that existed as a result of denominational loyalty served as a foundation for a stable world in which people could count on friendships that endured over a lifetime. Emerging generations, however, tend to have much less invested in any particular denomination than older generations do, viewing churches—to the extent they're interested in church at all—through the consumerist lens of cost-benefit analysis. They care much less about denominational history or doctrinal purity. As a result, they certainly seem to care less (shockingly so, to longtime denominational stalwarts) about the survival of the traditional denominational bureaucracies that underlie mission work and educational initiatives.

A Conversation (Brief Interlude)

I had a conversation recently with the new co-chairs of our outreach ministry. Both women had joined our church and our denomination within the last five years. As we reviewed the budget, one woman looked up and said, "What is this line item?"

"Oh, that's the money we send to the denomination," I answered.

"Really?" she said. "That seems like an awful lot. It's over half of our outreach budget. What do they do with that money?"

"Well, that money goes to support the mission work of the denomination."

"*All* that money goes toward mission?"

I was getting a little uncomfortable. "Not in the strictest sense, no."

"In what sense then?"

"Part of it goes to overseas mission. Part of it goes to mission here in the U.S., our advocacy for justice, support for ministries of compassion. Part goes to education. Part goes to support ministerial search and call. Part comes back to the region. Part goes to cover the administrative costs."

"Sounds to me like a big chunk of it goes to paying people's salaries to administer programs that have nothing to do with the kind of ministry we're trying to do right here."

Really uncomfortable, I said, "Look, we have a historic commitment to support the initiatives of our denomination. That's just the way it works."

"Fine. So, what do we get in return?"

"Lots of stuff."

"Like what?"

"Well, we get the satisfaction of supporting and belonging to something on a national, even a global level."

"Hmmm … I'd like the satisfaction of actually doing ministry. That's a lot of money for something that sounds curiously like institutional maintenance. Just think of the amazing things we could do right here with that kind of money."

"You're just going to have to trust me on this one. Ask _____ and _____. They've been around forever. They'll tell you we've got to do this."

Part of the reason we are in a post-denominational world, and part of the challenge facing mainline denominations going forward, is wrapped up in that discussion. It's going to be harder and harder to make that argument to people who have no broader sense of the scope and breadth of denominational history or its current vision for mission. As _____ and _____ grow older and become less involved in the life of the congregation, the people capable of making the argument for maintaining the institution will be fewer and fewer.

Couple that with emerging generations that have very little denominational loyalty and very little in the way of an impulse to join institutions, and you have a recipe for increasing difficulty for denominational survival—if what you mean by survival has to do with maintaining structures with their administrative and personnel costs.

Back to Congregations in a Post-Denominational World

In the denominational world where mainliners held sway, older generations often saw participation in the church as a necessity for salvation, as a way to get involved in a worthy cause, or as a socially approved activity. In other words, the church was viewed as instrumentally useful in the service of larger projects (i.e., getting to heaven, doing the work of compassion and justice, networking, etc.), and friendship was an outgrowth of associating with other people to achieve these other ends.

Older generations, because society and one's social networks tended to be more stable, could count on friendships that endured over a lifetime due to proximity. You could make friends in kindergarten, graduate from high school, and go to work together in the factory, mine, or quarry. If you didn't work together, you went to work on the farm, and your friend started up down at the family drug store in your hometown. Or, if everyone went to college, you and your childhood friends often returned home to set up shop, hang out a shingle, or join a practice among the same familiar faces. You could often count on knowing the same people, having the same friends over the course of your life. Chances are that, after having grown up, you belonged to the same church you and your family had always attended.

In other words, older generations didn't need the church to make friends; they already had a whole network of friendships developed early on. People could join churches based on a variety of factors—denominational loyalty, worship style, doctrinal purity, commitment to justice, or connectedness to desirable social networks—and trust that friendship was available, whether from the institution or among their antecedent social networks. I call this *affiliate community*. People affiliate with a group based on some prior commitment to an ideal or project.

"You guys do VBS? Great! My kids are little hellions."

From these affiliations community can grow as people join together around some higher calling.

"This place is great! I see your kids are hellions, too. Maybe we could get them together while we go to Krav Maga. It's the official self-defense system of the

Israeli Defense Forces, you know."

That's not to say that older generations didn't make friends at church via affiliate community; they did. Recognizing the implicit expectations of social stability among older generations, however, helps to point up the different need the church fulfilled in the past. Church, for older generations, is where you go to get stuff done, and if you make friends along the way, so much the better. But if you can't count on social stability to make and keep friends, the church becomes a different kind of place altogether.

Young adults, because they live in a world where social stability can no longer be assumed, need to be more creative about developing and sustaining personal relationships. I call this kind of association *attachment community,* where people come together because of a need to attach themselves to a group of people for the purpose of cultivating friendship.

"You guys drink beer? Outside of work, I don't really know anybody in this city. I've got to find some people to hang out with. Otherwise, I think I'm going to go Krav Maga on somebody. It's the official self-defense system of the Israeli Defense Forces, you know."

The church has an opportunity in this itinerant culture to be a place for making friends.

"That's not what the church is for."

Why not?

"Because, the church has more serious business to attend to than whether some young person has anybody to go bowling with on Friday night."

The smart-aleck response that comes to mind is: "Really? How's that working out for you? Got young people knocking down your doors to get in?"

The more measured response is: "Perhaps, the church in a post-denominational world needs to imagine itself differently. Instead of understanding itself as an institution that needs to attract people to get things done, it should begin to see itself as a gathering where God promises to be, and where people can flourish as the communal beings God created them to be."

"A gathering where God promises to be, where people can flourish as the communal beings God created them to be." What do I mean by that? The gathering, of course, has to do with the deep yearning for community I have been describing. The purpose of this gathering is to draw people God loves together so that they can draw strength from one another as they seek to find their lives, which allows them not only to live but to thrive.

"Put that way, the whole thing sounds like another attempt to use the church to meet individual needs—in this case, the need for community."

I can see how it might first appear that way. Bear with me a moment and let me see if I can be more clear about this. The kind of reorientation of purpose I am describing—one that views the church first as a gathering seeking to live out its purpose as human beings created for friendship in community—I think more nearly describes the kind of church described, for example, in Acts 2:44–47:

> All who believed were together and had all things in common; they would sell their possessions and goods and distribute the proceeds to all, as any had need. Day by day, as they spent much time together in the temple, they broke break together at home and ate their food with glad and generous hearts, praising God and having the good will of all the people. And day by day the Lord added to their number those who were being saved.

Now, it may very well be that this earliest description of the church is nostalgic, an idealized account of something that never really existed, except in the imaginations of those who longed for a church that only seemed possible in simpler times. This charge is not particularly damaging to what I'm trying to describe, however, because the "ideal" is precisely what I'm after. If the question is "What should the church be?" it seems plausible to go back to the earliest idealized accounts of what the church was *supposed* to look like—at least in the minds of its earliest supporters.

The idealized church in Acts 2 describes a group of people, the primary description of which underscores the desire to be "together." The impulse to congregate makes a great deal of sense for the early church when you consider that this newfound faith left them at odds both with the Jewish faith of their childhood (which very often meant from their families and friends) and with a hostile political culture (which had just made a political example of their leader/rabbi by a very public execution).

Moreover, the author of Acts draws attention to their common life together, characterized by their willingness to share everything. When referring to this passage, many commentators focus on the economic component, particularly the phrase indicating that the community, which "had all things in common," would "sell their possessions and goods and distribute the proceeds to all, as any had need." This inclination to pool their goods is extremely important and shouldn't be glossed over. However, I think the passage is speaking about more than just the willingness of the early church to run church sanctioned yard sales. Sharing all things in common apparently also included their time and their affection for one another. The text continues, pointing out that "day by day, as they spent much time together in the temple, they broke bread at home and ate their food with glad and generous hearts, praising God and having the good will of all the people." In other words, they became friends. They hung out together. They ate food together. They sought one another's company.

What came out of all this congregating? That is to say, what is the progression of events set down by the author of Acts? Those who believed came together. They shared a common life, including their resources, their time, and their affection. They spent "much time together," breaking bread and enjoying one another. Out of all this togetherness emerged two things: worship and expansion.

It seems important to note that worship appears, at least in part, to be the communal response to God's having called these people to share "much time together." Having broken bread together with "glad and generous hearts," the first thing the author of Acts says they do is start "praising God." Worship, at least in this telling of it, breaks forth from a people who love each other and take every opportunity to be together.

What happens next? People see all of this comity and friendship and fall all over themselves to be a part of it. The opportunity to make friends, to find shelter from an often hostile world, to be a part of a community held together by something greater than a collection of individual interests appears so attractive that "day by day" new people show up and want in. In this way, the church isn't just a collection of individuals seeking to get their social needs met; it's a *polis* that helps people to identify what their truest needs are.

It strikes me that the church today might take its cue from this earliest idealized description of the church.

What Do I Envision?

As a young man set down in the mountains of East Tennessee, I experienced the dislocation that came as a result of following my vocation. Though I was doing what I wanted to do, I felt a deep need to belong to something. My marriage was still too new and unformed to be thrown back on itself as the only system of social and emotional support. I needed a place, a group of people to whom I could belong, and with whom my young wife and I could share our lives. My wife and I found this refuge among our friends at Aunt B's. Having that kind of communal grounding freed me up to explore who I was supposed to be and what it was that I had the gifts to do.

In a mobile society I believe the church needs to begin to think first about how to bring people together to cultivate relationships that are difficult to form as people grow older. That is not to say that churches need to leave behind their commitment to worshiping God or to seeking justice or to educating and forming the faithful. It is to say that those things can be the *product* of communities called together by God rather than places that seek to form communities for the purpose of accomplishing those things.

Am I saying it's wrong to gather people together to accomplish some greater goal or that working together can't produce community? Absolutely not. At times when people can assume a stable culture where friendship and community are durable products of being located in a single place over time, I think affiliate community can work just fine. But in a time when the culture seems to force dislocation and rootlessness, when friendships are often fleeting and difficult to cultivate, being a place where the initial appeal revolves around getting things done is going to be a hard sell to emerging generations.

Something like a pub or coffee house ministry—almost cliché in some circles and misunderstood in others—if not viewed as just another slick marketing tool to bait and switch a desirable demographic into the church, have the virtue of providing non-threatening space in which people can gather to make friends. The focus is first focused on creating space and not on creating new members.

"Fine. But what if those people don't ever join the church?"

What if they don't? They weren't scratching and clawing to get in anyway. Why not just do this because it's the right thing to do? People who have no other community need a place to belong. Whether the church ever benefits from it, why not just provide it as a service because we've been called to minister to a world struggling to keep its head above water?

In a post-denominational world, the church is going to have to learn to love ministry, service, loving people because that's what we were created and called by God to do. It should quit spending all its time figuring out all the angles by which it might benefit from ministry. Ministry is not a marketing tool, designed to sell something; it's a vocation, a way of life.

Oh, you may believe that it's all about helping people, but if you go into it thinking that you might get members out of it, you're selling something—at least that's how emerging generations tend to experience it.

The problem is that the marketing that worked so well on Baby Boomers feels plastic and inauthentic to emerging generations—the most targeted marketing demographic in the history of the world. They've been pitched in so many ingenious and edgy ways, they can smell a sales job from a mile away. They tend to be not so much immune to slick marketing as repulsed by it. To a generation that grew up watching TV and engaging the world online, attempts to package important things (e.g., love, family, faith, patriotism, etc.) via slick marketing sound contrived and hollow.

Hint: If you think your only problem is finding the right marketing angle to attract young people, the best you can hope for is ironic engagement with people who think you're lame.

The message they hear from churches that do ministry with a view to attracting them is "We want to help ... especially if it means you'll buy what we're selling." It's like a bread crumb trail you lay out there in the hope that what you're offering is so enticing, people won't notice where it leads until they look up and find themselves in the sanctuary, having filled out a pledge card. All I'm saying is that people used to ingenious sales tactics can sniff the breadcrumb trail out with amazing olfactory dexterity.

"That's not true. We really do want to help. So what if we also want people to join?"

I know it doesn't feel right thinking of it as a sales job, but that's what it is. You're saying: "Look at us. We do good things. We've got a great thing in here. You should come in and see. Trust us. You'll like it."

Congregations have oriented themselves that way over the years.

- You're out there.

- We think you should be in here.

- Our job is to figure out how to get you to decide to leave "out there" and come "in here" with us.

I don't think there's any way to lay out the breadcrumb trail without setting up the relationship as salesperson/customer. It's a war of escalating strategies concerned with marketing and marketing resistance. Most churches are trying to figure out newer and more subtle ways to offer a product, hoping that in the process people won't recognize it's a sales job and will buy what we're selling.

Field Notes

- What if we oriented ourselves the other way around?

- What if, instead of exerting more and more energy trying to design newer and more undetectable sales strategies so that people would come in and join us, we started pouring our energy into figuring out newer and more creative ways to go outside—no strings attached— just because that's where Jesus is?

- What if we quit worrying about swelling the membership rolls?

- What if we trust that our faithfulness is an end in itself, that following Jesus is what we're called to do, not just something we do to bring people in here?

- What if we gave without expecting anything in return?

Don't kid yourself. People can tell when there are strings attached.

Maybe if people came to believe that we weren't just doing nice stuff "out there" to entice them to come "in here," maybe if we showed more interest in getting to know people where they live instead of trying to get them to come live with us, people might not run the other way screaming when they hear somebody say "Jesus."

Whether or not denominations survive intact should be of less concern to us than that the gospel is lived out. And if our highest priority is living out the gospel, then we're going to have to spend more time thinking about how we can produce great and interesting ministry out of the stable foundation of community and less time worrying about how to prop up flagging institutions.

The beauty of Aunt B's is that it doesn't cost anything but time.

9

"Going Green...All the Cool Kids Are Doing It" or Ecologically Concerned

"You Mean Everything?"

As a freshman in Bible college I took an introductory course entitled "Bible Survey." As the name suggests, we started at the beginning in Genesis and worked our way through the whole Bible over the course of a year. I remember being fairly self-assured about the positions I had come to school with—after all, I came from a family of ministers. I was a two-time sword drill champion at vacation Bible school, and camper-of-the-week at church camp my sophomore year of high school. I figured I'd pretty well locked up the basics. Bible college was only a way to fill in the details.

In the second week of classes, my professor Walt Zorn completely altered my fundamental understanding of creation. I had always assumed the crown-of-creation, humans-have-been-given-dominion position. I lived my life as though the planet had been given to us to dispose of as we please. God created it for us, and our only responsibility for it was not to screw it up so bad we couldn't inhabit it any longer. It never occurred to me to think that God might actually have some attachment to this stuff. I thought of creation in purely utilitarian terms.

Imagine my shock, then, when Dr. Zorn said, "God created all this simply because God loves to create; which means God loves all of it—you, me, the birds, the trees, the pond on the eastern edge of campus, and the cockroaches in the music hall." I got the "you" and "me" part. In fact, I even sort of shallowly assumed the "birds," "trees," and "the pond" part. But the "cockroaches" thing really threw me.

How could God love cockroaches? Mosquitos? Poodles?

This required some reflection. If God could love those things—things God had presumably created and called good—could God also love things like dental plaque, rabies viruses, and the St. Louis Cardinals? As a Chicago Cubs fan and heretofore only casual tooth brusher, I found this thought terribly unsettling. What kind of God creates these things—and then proceeds to call them good, even to love them? If this was true, I thought to myself, God is much scarier and much more interesting than I ever believed. Why? Well, it certainly opened up my understanding of the breadth of God's capacity to love. I assumed God loved me ... or *even* me (as I would have been prone to phrasing it, because of the self-imposed modesty appropriate to all good Evangelicals). But in believing that, I didn't feel like God really had that big a job. As with many adolescents, I confronted the world with the secret belief that I was pretty much what God had been aiming for in the whole creation thing all along. Of course, I maintained enough humility to pay lip service to the fact that "I certainly wasn't perfect." On the whole, though, it didn't occur to me that God's love for me was a particularly heavy lift.

As I started to consider the scope of God's love in relationship to creation, however, a window opened up to me about the radical nature of this whole God thing. God *loves* all this stuff. God loves *all* this stuff—not just the stuff I love, but also the stuff I fail to notice, the stuff I dismiss, the stuff I hate. I found the whole idea rather bracing. If God loves everything God has created, what should my relationship to it be?

Given my own deplorable self-preoccupation, I had grown up believing that the non-human part of creation was window-dressing, created for either the use or delight of humans. In other words, I had no need to worry myself about the fate of creation, because what was important wasn't creation but humanity—the crown jewel sitting in the midst of it all.

I had seen the commercial with the native-American man standing with a tear rolling down the side of his face at the side of the highway as a bag of garbage thrown from a passing car lands at his feet. I got the message. We were supposed to "give a hoot!" and not pollute. I learned from Smokey the Bear that only *I* could "prevent forest fires." In other words, I got the popular ecological message designed to socialize the post-Baby Boom, Gen-X generation. It was snappy, well thought-out. I still remember the taglines.

Unfortunately, what I didn't learn was how that message of ecological conservation made any appreciable difference to my faith. In my mind I learned through the commercials and public service announcements that pollution was wrong because it was a self-defeating form of nest-fouling that would eventually affect how my generation and generations to follow would be able to live on the planet. I never made the connection that maybe God, having organized this whole party, might have an opinion about the despoliation of the dance floor. It wasn't until I heard somebody say out loud that God might just care about the rest of creation that I began to think that my relationship to the faith I'd absorbed from early on might have a more cosmic scope than the size and sincerity of my heart; which is to say, maybe God had bigger fish to fry than just me.

I take it that since my early brushes with environmental awareness young people have gotten a steadier and more profoundly connected understanding of the importance of creation as an end in itself, and not just as a playground for bored middle-class white suburbanites. The whole thing unnerved me.

This chapter offers a look at creation, which emerging generations believe involves not only practical questions about economic impact or personal enjoyment but also moral questions that go to the very heart of our purpose and destiny. In this chapter I make the case that mainline denominations, which have displayed some sympathies for environmental concerns, have the potential to offer leadership by helping people think through the moral and theological implications of how we care for God's creation, and why, beyond self-preservation, we might want to do so in the first place.

Caring about Creation Isn't Just a Marketing Strategy

As I waited for my coffee to quit brewing this morning, I decided to go outside to get the paper. On the front page was this headline: "Excessive Heat: Triple-Digit Records Falling with Regularity in Louisville." That sounds about right. It's been blisteringly hot this summer.

The rise in temperature (we had a 90-degree day in March, in Louisville!) during the summer of 2012 elicits great anxiety over the prospect of climate change (http://www.cbsnews.com/8301–18563_162–57466244/heat-wave-raises-warning-signs-for-climate-change-scientists/). Have we emitted so much carbon dioxide into the atmosphere that we have irreparably damaged our world? Apart from the increase in greenhouse gases, there are issues involving the air we breathe, the food we eat, and the water we drink. Have human beings traded the ease of technological convenience for a potentially unlivable planet one day down the road?

"That's just hippy alarmism."

The data seem fairly clear that we have profoundly damaged the earth, which was a gift to us from those who went before. I think that assertion holds up with little credible opposition. Importantly for the church, emerging generations find the prospect of a despoiled planet alarming. Emerging generations expect to be involved in making the world greener.[1]

The range of environmental concerns has expanded since they first appeared as a popular issue in the 1960s. Early on, environmentalism was preoccupied with the problems of pollution—largely air, water, and litter. Much of the early emphasis had to do with ecology, the study of "interactions between individual organisms and their environments" (http://plato.stanford.edu/entries/ecology/). Since then, environmental concern has taken on a more global flavor, however, with the onset of disquiet about "global warming," which lately has shifted to a more precise descriptor, "climate change." The claim of climate change scientists is that humans, through their production of greenhouse gases, are affecting the world's climate, making it detectably warmer. Now the problem is more than just pollution, which soils the earth we live in, making it less habitable as a result of the dirtiness; it's the global effects of soiling the earth that offer up nightmare scenarios to those who are paying attention.

Young people, protestations of generational narcissism to the contrary notwithstanding, are paying attention. And why wouldn't they? The younger you are, the more stake you've got in what the world's going to look like in 25, 50, 75 years.

The church, which has its own theological stake in the discussion about providing stewardship to the good gift of creation—more about that in a

---

[1]Much attention has been given to a now infamous study by Jean Twenge: "Generational Differences in Young Adults' Life Goals, Concern for Others, and Civic Orientation, 1966–2009," Jean M. Twenge, PhD, and Elise C. Freeman, MA, San Diego State University; W. Keith Campbell, PhD, University of Georgia; Journal of Personality and Social Psychology, Vol. 102, No. 5. In this study, Dr. Twenge and her colleagues suggest that commitment to the environment steadily declines from Baby-Boomers to Millennials. However, both the methodology of the study and the interpretation of the data have been strenuously disputed. See Mike Hais and Morley Winograd, "Millennials Are a 'We' not 'Me' Generation, http://mikeandmorley.com/wordpress/?p=99, March 15, 2012, or for a meta-disputation of Twenge's claims calling on various studies and articles, see Rachel Tardiff and Whit Jones, "Twenge Youth Study on Environment is Total Sham," http://www.energyactioncoalition.org/press-release/twenge-youth-study-environment-total-sham, March 16, 2012. I find the case against Twenge's methodology and conclusions persuasive.

moment—would do well to pay attention to the rising anxiety about what we're doing to the world.

"Are you saying Christians should think green because it will attract young people? That's pretty cynical."

Good question. No, I don't think attracting young people should lead the church to take climate change seriously anymore than I think jiggering your worship service to focus on "cool people" singing "cool songs" in anticipation of an ecclesiastical hipster offering a glib and inoffensive talk on "Godly time management" is the answer. Christian faithfulness isn't an evangelistic tool; it's a way of being that communicates a commitment to the radically subversive reign of God. Christians, as Stanley Hauerwas has said before, have a way of speaking about nature: We call it creation. That is to say, Christians believe that God has a hand in all this.

Mainline denominations have shown some sensitivity to the issues surrounding the environment, which puts them a step or two ahead of most of their counterparts in the Evangelical wing of Christianity, which has often tended to find itself aligned with the Republican Party, and therefore, at odds with scientific consensus on issues ranging from evolution to climate change.

While I think that, in many respects, a generalized view of Evangelicalism as anti-science is an unfair caricature, it is a common enough stereotype that it seems important to name. The conventional assumptions about Evangelical reticence on these scientific issues leaves a door open to mainline denominations.

Emerging generations, which have largely grown up hearing about the Enlightenment triumph of reason in science and technology, are put off by what they perceive to be the anti-intellectualism of more conservative Christian traditions. According to the most recent polling by the Pew Forum on Religion, a significant demographic shift is taking place among emerging generations and their religious commitments.

The growth in the number of religiously unaffiliated Americans—sometimes called the rise of the "nones"—is largely driven by generational replacement, the gradual supplanting of older generations by newer ones. A third of adults under 30 have no religious affiliation (32%), compared with just one in ten who are 65 and older (9%) [http://www.pewforum.org/Unaffiliated/nones-on-the-rise.aspx]. And young adults today are much more likely to be unaffiliated than previous generations were at a similar stage in their lives. The reason for this shift in religious commitment, I have no doubt, has a number of reasons. However, when I speak with my students they are generally very clear about their belief that religion and science occupy different spheres. Their attitudes speak fairly clearly about which sphere they think bears the highest authority. Science, they've learned, is the sphere of "facts," while religion relies on "opinions."

Consequently, when emerging generations sense a confrontation between a religion that denies scientific commonplaces like evolution and global climate change, they opt for what they believe to be the facts of science. Mainliners have an opportunity to reestablish the initiative with young people by demonstrating an unapologetic embrace of scientific consensus.

However, it occurs to me that mainline denominations need to take seriously their role not just in parroting progressive positions on the environment but in articulating a theological understanding of why it is that Christians have a real stake in caring for creation. Why, in other words, do mainliners believe God cares about creation, and therefore, why should we?

Nature, as it is commonly spoken of, is a force all its own, a potential rival to God. Without claiming that God zapped everything into being over the course of one amazingly productive work week, or that God pulls all the mechanical levers, Christians can still believe that God is in the middle of a dynamic process whereby what is has come into being under God's loving attention—and that "what is" is what Christians call creation.

Now, it might seem unimportant to distinguish between nature and creation, but a lot turns on the distinction. Nature is too thin a concept for Christians, because nature operates too easily as an abstraction over against which humans are often pitted. Humans versus Nature. On this reading, nature is a thing we need—as much as we are able—to direct, to save, to control, to bless, to outwit. In other words, nature is something humans must confront as an independent reality.

On the other hand, Christians take creation to be an expression of God's desire. If God is in the middle of all that is, and if God loves and calls good all that has come from God, then we can begin to understand a bit more about God's character by attending to creation. The character of the relationship between humans and "what is" is seriously altered by seeing ourselves as but another facet of God's self-expression—an important facet, if Genesis is to be believed, but still only a part of God's larger whole.

Moreover, since God expresses Godself through creation, we can begin to get an idea of what God desires, but also of God's patience in getting what God wants. God is perfectly willing to let time shape and mold what God has made. It seems to me that this is one advantage of following the consensus scientific position of evolution, and one more in line with the God we find in Scripture: God need not zap everything into existence fully formed, but shows an amazing degree of patience in allowing creation to unfold over billions of years.

The net effect of understanding creation as a demonstration of God's patience is that those who would be true to such a God must consider patience, rather than explicit and overwhelming displays of power, to be a virtue. Without setting down a whole theology of creation, this view of God's patience perfectly aligns with the eschatological nature of Christianity. That is to say, Christianity understands God to be working in time to establish God's reign, displaying an amazing amount of patience with and trust in God's people to accomplish God's purposes. Mainline denominations would do well to see patience as the virtue that manifests the hope that God—and not our amazingly clever selves—is in charge.

Every parent knows, for example, that it would be much easier to go into your kid's room and remove the toxic waste hidden under the bed, or the biological cultures growing in the laundry pile. But good parents don't do all the work, refuse to smooth out every bump, believing that the result of waiting and trusting will produce more fruit in the long run.

But as the Age of Enlightenment gave way to the Age of Invention and Industry, the need for patience seemed less necessary. Our ability to iron out the wrinkles of an inscrutable universe gave us great power. Economic and political growth in the early days of the United States were spurred on by innovation, much of it technological. Three notable inventions drove economic expansion: gas lighting, the steam-powered locomotive, and the telegraph. These allowed us to live farther apart, but required a new set of dependencies.

Energy, which had prior to the Industrial Revolution been dependent on the nature of its renewability, became something that could be mined and tapped from ancient stockpiles. In other words, energy had for the most part always been something that we harvested or attempted to direct its flow— we cut it down, we picked it up, we caught it in sails, and we channeled its powers to turn mills (Sachs, 35). In short, we used energy sources that, given a short passage of time, would be there again and again. The Industrial Revolution, on the other hand, put us on the path with proportionally cheaper costs on the front end—that is, pound for pound non-renewable resources like coal, oil, and gas were more efficient, and therefore, cheaper to use than their organic counterparts. The long-term cost horizon for non-renewables, however, was much more expensive—at least with respect to the cost incurred by the damage to creation.

Ironically then, the very energy technologies that gave us a measure of independence, by allowing us to live farther from one another while still maintaining contact, made us more dependent on technologies of energy production over which the individual had much less control. And the need for patience took a back seat to our belief that we could engineer any reality that suited us. In the process, our dependence on God became an abstraction, removed from our everyday experience of the world. What do we need God for when we have General Electric and Johnson & Johnson?

Recovering Eden by Assault

For a long time now we have understood ourselves as traveling toward some sort of industrial paradise, some new Eden conceived and constructed entirely by human ingenuity. And we have thought ourselves free to use and abuse nature in any way that might further this enterprise. Now we face overwhelming evidence that we are not smart enough to recover Eden by assault, and that nature does not tolerate or excuse abuses. If in spite of the evidence against us, we are finding it hard to relinquish our old ambition, we are also seeing more clearly every day how that ambition has reduced and enslaved us. We see how everything—the whole world—is belittled by the idea that all creation is moving or ought to move toward an end that some body, some human body, has thought up. To be free of that end and that ambition would be a delightful and precious thing. Once free of it, we might again go about our work and our lives with a seriousness and pleasure denied to us when we merely submit to a fate already determined by gigantic politics, economics, and technology.

WENDELL BERRY, *WHAT ARE PEOPLE FOR?*, 209-10

For the creation waits with eager longing for the revealing of the children of God; for the creation was subjected to futility, not of its own will but by the will of the one who subjected it, in hope that the creation itself will be set free from its bondage to decay and will obtain the freedom of the glory of the children of God. We know that the whole creation has been groaning in labor pains until now; and not only the creation, but we ourselves who have the first fruits of the Spirit, groan inwardly while we wait for adoption, the redemption of our bodies. (Romans 8:19-23)

I must confess that environmentalism has not traditionally been one of the issues about which I have generally gotten exercised. Part of the reason I'm not usually attuned to environmental issues is that I'm so deeply entrenched in an economic system that causes those problems; and quite frankly, I like the convenience it affords me. Oh, I try to do my own small part. But when it comes right down to making decisions, concern for creation has not usually ranked high on the list of criteria I use to decide. I am, when I'm honest with myself, more a part of the problem than the solution in this case.

The problem for me, though, is that I know my inattention to creation is merely a matter of convenience, not a matter of a studied reflection on discipleship. I claim to live by the conviction that the determinative factor in my life is my attachment to the community of Jesus followers; I am a part of a group of pilgrims whose lives are shaped by their relationship to Jesus. But when it concerns creation, I have conveniently exempted myself from having to take my faith seriously in making decisions that impact the very world for which Christ died, and that's not right.

Unfortunately, however, creation is not something we find ourselves in; it's something of which we're inextricably a part. As Wendell Berry says, "It is not a place into which we reach from some safe standpoint outside it. We are in it and are a part of it while we use it. If it does not thrive, we cannot thrive" (Berry, 208-9). The future into which followers of Jesus are walking isn't a private future where humans are individually cared for without reference to anything else. Our future is much more organic than that—quite literally more *organic*; which is to say, whatever the reign of God looks like as it comes to be fully realized, it will unfold in conjunction with God's creation, not independent of it.

"For the creation waits with eager longing for the revealing of the children of God," Paul says. He seems to be talking about what Ireneaus called the recapitulation of creation, in which everything will be redeemed in the end by Christ and his return in glory. But I also think Paul is talking about our inexorable relationship to that which God has created right now. Perhaps creation "waits with eager longing for the revealing of the children of God," not just at some eschatological point in the future. Perhaps creation "waits with eager longing for" the children of God to take seriously their link with God's creation right now. Perhaps it's not enough to admit that we're a part of the problem; maybe what is necessary as followers of Jesus is to begin taking seriously our responsibilities as providers of hope for the world in the present by the way we make decisions right now.

If as followers of Jesus, Christ ought to be the ultimate shaper of our lives, then even little decisions about our relationship to creation have eternal implications. The only Eden we care anything about isn't one we could recover by assault anyway.

Field Notes

- Do the obvious things like limit paper use and disposable cups and utensils. (Recycle, of course.)

- Go to an email newsletter. (They're free and pretty! Try Mailchimp. com.)

- Do an energy audit. (Check out the feasibility of solar, geo-thermal, and green roofs when it's time to upgrade.)

- If you've got extra space, offer it to your neighborhood for a community garden or a farmers market.

- Encourage car-pooling and limit the number of meetings. (Hint: This is a good idea anyway.)

10

"How About, You Know... the Gays?"

How Is Kirby?

Apart from the yearly drag show on Phil Donahue, I had no contact with gay people as a kid. That's not true, exactly, because as we know now, gay people are always around; I just didn't know that then.

The whole thought of people loving others of the same gender was unfathomable to me as a child. I knew it was wrong, but I'm not sure *how* I knew. I don't remember having a conversation about it with anybody. It wasn't the kind of conversation we would have had—like we would never talk about the relative advantages of owning a beach house in the Keys over owning a sailboat in Martha's Vineyard. What would have been the point? Our lives were never going to be touched by it, so why talk about it? I don't know if I just picked up a vibe about it when my parents seemed a little fidgety if we walked in and saw Billy Crystal on *Soap*. It could be that I, like every kid my age, was especially familiar with the schoolyard epithets that made their way into our vocabulary as a means of publicly establishing our masculinity. I don't know where I learned it, but I knew being homosexual was a bad thing for people to be. I didn't have to do any soul searching about the issue. I was pretty certain that the whole idea was self-evidently something that any "normal" person could recognize as abhorrent—and by "normal" I meant something like "Christian" (since Christianity was a normative reality in my world).

We now live in a different world from the one in which I grew up. My kids have grown up with children who have two moms and two dads.

Our own minds, my wife's and mine, have changed over the years regarding this issue. I know that on the rare occasion when we talked about "Charlie's" moms with our children, we were adamant that love is love, and that "Charlie's moms love each other like Mommy and Daddy do." But we never had sit-down lessons on diversity. Consequently, when my own kids, who are now teenagers, overhear the debate about same gender marriage, they're confounded. Why is this such a big deal?

I grew up in the aftermath of the Civil Rights movement believing that everybody is created equal, regardless of race. Just a few years before I came onto the scene, however, no consensus existed on the issue. People braved batons and German Shepherds, went to jail, lost their jobs, and died in the streets to establish an understanding of human relationships that I have always taken to be self-evident. It never occurred to me as a child that anyone still believed that black people were inferior. I didn't carry the same baggage about the issue of race that my parent's generation had had to haul around the first part of their lives.

Let me be quick to add that passing the Civil Rights Act didn't do away with the baggage from my parents' and grandparents' generations, but it did at least two things that I can see: (1) it made continuing to hold racist beliefs problematic, and (2) it cleared the cultural air so that continuing to indoctrinate children with racist ideas was not only problematic socially, but also more difficult.

These days, my children don't have to carry around the same baggage I did on the issue of lesbian, gay, bisexual, and transgender (LGBT) people. They see the propriety of love as an issue unencumbered by concerns about which genders should be paired together and which pairings should be avoided at all costs.

I'm aware that there are more initials for intersex, queer, questioning, and so on. I am also fully aware that "gay" is insufficient, since it doesn't account for things like Transgender and Intersex. I will sometimes use "gay" and LGBT in this chapter as a placeholder for "sexual orientation and gender identity" with full knowledge that I'm not adequately accounting for significant constituencies in this matter. To have to name constantly every possible constellation of orientation and identity would be literarily unwieldy. Therefore, I beg the forbearance of those I do not name explicitly each time.

A demographic divide over the issue of homosexuality has emerged, a divide that continues to grow wider with each passing day. The younger you are, the more likely you are to have no problem with the idea of a man marrying a man, a woman marrying a woman, or a man born in a woman's body, becoming what she feels she was created to be, and so on.

Just yesterday I had to come home to tell my children that Charlie died (a different Charlie). Charlie had been ordained in the church I pastored back in the '70s. He soon left the ministry, however, after meeting Kirby—the love of his life. In fact, he didn't last long in the church altogether. He just couldn't take being told that being gay made him unacceptable. Charlie became a corporate executive and moved to Virginia.

After Charlie retired, he and Kirby moved back to Louisville. They've been together over thirty-eight years. A former minister at our church got in touch with Charlie and encouraged him to come back to check out the church that had ordained him so many years before. He did. Charlie found that much had changed since he left. For one thing, our church had voted unanimously the year before to welcome all people, regardless of sexual orientation or gender identity, into full participation in the life and ministry of the church. He loved it and eventually rejoined.

However, not only did Charlie reconnect with the "kids" from his old youth group (almost all of whom were now parents and grandparents), but he got to know the youth who are in the church today. He talked to them, joked with them, brought donuts for them—in short, he cared about them. Everyone in our church, but especially the youth, loved Charlie.

Charlie died yesterday. I had to come home to tell my children. They cried. But their first question was, "How is Kirby?"

According to the statistics, the younger you are, the more likely the first question out of your mouth in a situation like this is "How is Kirby?" Because to young people Charlie and Kirby aren't first, gay men; they're people who've spent most of their lives loving and taking care of each other.

In a post-denominational world, mainline denominations are going to have to come to terms with the inevitability of having to appeal to young people whose first question upon hearing of the death of someone like Charlie is "How is Kirby?"

The Church Hates Gay People

- Almost 6 in 10 Americans (58%) believe homosexuality should be accepted by society (http://www.pewresearch.org/2011/05/13/most-say-homosexuality-should-be-accepted-by-society/).

- Of those people under age 50, 63% believe homosexuality should be accepted by society—under 30, 69% (http://www.pewresearch. org/2011/05/13/most-say-homosexuality-should-be-accepted-by-society/).

- Among all Americans, 64% believe that same gender relationships ought to be socially acceptable (http://publicreligion.org/research/2011/08/ generations-at-odds/).

- With the exception of white evangelicals, a majority of Americans who claim some religious affiliation believe that same-gender relationships ought to be socially acceptable (http://publicreligion. org/research/2011/08/generations-at-odds/).

- 54% believe same-gender marriage should be viewed as legally valid, an increase of 10% over the four-year period between June 2008 and May 2012. (http://politicalticker.blogs.cnn.com/2012/06/06/cnn-poll-americans-attitudes-toward-gay-community-changing/).

- 64% of people under 30 support same-sex marriage, while only 27% of those 70 and older are in favor of it (http://news.uchicago.edu/ article/2011/09/28/americans-move-dramatically-toward-acceptance-homosexuality-survey-finds).

- 65% of white mainline Protestants believe homosexuality should be accepted rather than discouraged (http://www.pewresearch.org/2011/05/ 13/most-say-homosexuality-should-be-accepted-by-society/).

- "There is at least a 20-point generation gap between Millennials (age 18 to 29) and seniors (age 65 and older) on every public policy measure in the survey concerning rights for gay and lesbian people." (http://publicreligion.org/research/2011/08/generations-at-odds/)

- A 2011 Public Religion Research Institute survey found that "nearly seven in ten (69%) Millennials agree that religious groups are alienating young people by being too judgmental about gay and lesbian issues" (http://publicreligion.org/research/2011/08/generations-at-odds/).

- "Born again Christians are more likely to disapprove of homosexuality than divorce" (Kinnaman and Lyons, 94).

David Kinnaman and Gabe Lyons, Evangelical authors of Unchristian: What a New Generation Really Thinks about Christianity, have this to say (http:// www.qideas.org/essays/unchristian-change-the-perception.aspx?page=2) about just how people view the church when it comes to homosexuality:

Out of twenty attributes that we assessed, both positive and negative, as they related to Christianity, the perception of being antihomosexual was at the top of the list. More than nine out of ten Mosaic and Buster [what I've called "emerging generations"] outsiders (91 percent) said "antihomosexual" accurately describes present-day Christianity. And two-thirds of outsiders have very strong opinions about Christians in this regard, easily generating the largest group of vocal critics. When you introduce yourself as a Christian to a friend, neighbor, or business associate who is an outsider, you might as well have it tattooed on your arm: antihomosexual, gay-hater, homophobic. I doubt you think of yourself in these terms, but that's what outsiders think of you.

Whether it realizes it or not, the church has a problem. Emerging generations think the church hates gay people. Regardless of what you believe about homosexuality, young people, when they find out you're a Christian, already think they know how you feel about it.

Mainline Protestant denominations face the same problem of being labeled "antihomosexual." However, almost two-thirds of white mainline Protestants believe homosexuality ought to be accepted. In other words, mainliners are getting something of a bum rap when it comes to their views on homosexuality—at least when stacking how they *actually* feel against what outsiders *think* they feel.

I say "something of a bum rap," however, because mainline Protestants have created (or at least allowed to stand) the biggest part of their problem: They haven't been able to find a voice that adequately communicates their belief that God's love transcends all the ways people differ from one another. As a result, though a sizable majority agrees that homosexuality ought to be accepted rather than discouraged, emerging generations don't differentiate between mainliners and evangelicals when it comes to this issue.

At this point, someone will rightly point out that (65%) may represent a majority, but it stands a good ways from being a consensus. And as long as mainliners can't come to a consensus, they can't put themselves forward as supportive of the full inclusion of LGBT people; and this fact will continue to define mainline Protestants until they take intentional strides to address it.

But addressing it is difficult.

Let me stop here for a moment and clarify who my intended audience is for this section. I'm making some assumptions about you, dear reader, which I should put on the table:

- Taking into consideration the title of the book, you're probably a part of the Protestant mainline—although you may not be, which, frankly, would be a really great thing.

- You're probably anxious about the decline of the church in general and mainline denominations in particular.

- If you're still reading this far into the book, and if the statistics hold true, you probably agree that LGBT people ought to be accepted, both in society and in the church.

If, for some reason, you think LGBT people are sinners who shouldn't be allowed the privilege of full participation in the life and ministry of the church until such time as they can prove they are no longer LGB or T, then this part of the book is not for you. I'm writing at this point specifically to people who believe LGBT people should be accepted (even celebrated!) in the church, but who have yet to make that fact a practical focus of their lives and ministries.

Who am I specifically *not* addressing right now? I'm not trying to persuade those people who are convinced homosexuality is a sin that they're wrong. Though I disagree with them on this issue, I'm not sure there's anything I could write that would change their minds. So if that's you, you have my blessing to stop reading now.

If, on the other hand, you agree with me in principle about the inclusion of LGBT people, the rest of this chapter will be devoted to answering the common objections people raise to taking a public stance on the issue. If you agree that the statistics about trends in attitudes toward LGBT people do not bode well for the church in a post-denominational world, then this part is meant to persuade you that you need to say something.[1]

In a post-denominational world, the first thing people think when they hear that you're a Christian should not be "gay-hater." Whether the terminology is Open and Affirming, Reconciling, More Light, or Welcoming and Affirming, mainline denominations (and their congregations), given the trends, need to consider how they will extend hospitality to LGBT folks.

---

[1] I understand that I'm being polemical here. It would be disingenuous of me, however, if I acted as though I had no convictions on this subject that I thought were worth sharing. I am a preacher, which means that I'm not trying at this point to "make you think." I'm trying to persuade you to follow Jesus more faithfully. Now, you may not think what I'm arguing for is faithful at all, but merely an exercise in obfuscation or pettifogging. Fair enough. But at least we'll be clear where we stand. Sometimes that's the best you've got.

"We already have gay people in our church. Why do we need to go and make a big deal of it?"

I can't tell you how many times I have had this conversation. This most often occurs with leaders who, on an individual level, believe that LGBT people ought to be welcomed into the life of the church without any qualification of the kinds of ministry or service in which they might engage. These church leaders are sympathetic to the idea of Open and Affirming as a move the church needs to make ... some day down the road. They're "just not there yet."

Let me preface what I'm about to say with a nod toward the difficulty of negotiating the ecclesial waters. All churches are different, but they share enough in common that I know what I'm about to say is a difficult word to hear. Church leaders have to take into consideration a number of factors, not least of which for pastors is their livelihoods. As someone who very nearly lost his first job out of seminary over this very issue, and who had to leave another job over some principles on which I thought it necessary to take a stand, I'm well aware of the treacherous waters controversial issues can create. Having offered that disclaimer, let me jump in with both feet.

"We're just not there yet."

That can mean any number of things, from "There is a significant constituency within the church who are opposed to the idea of the full inclusion of gay people, and that's not going to change unless some people die or move on," to "We *used* to have a significant constituency within the church who were opposed to the idea of the full inclusion of gay people (we had a big blow up over it once) and we're afraid to open that can of worms again," to "I was a leader in a situation where a big fight over this issue occurred, and I don't ever want to go through that again," to "I really don't know how my people would respond to this issue, but the thought of having it cause dissension makes me uptight."

"We're just not there yet" can mean different things, depending on your situation. I don't know what it means for you, but *you* had better know ... and with some precision. If you believe that God wants LGBT individuals to be welcomed and affirmed in the church as a general rule, then you need to get a handle on why they're not welcomed and affirmed in your particular situation.

The important question, though, isn't "Do you know if you're supportive of gay people?" The really important question is "Do *gay people* know you're supportive of gay people?" It's an important distinction. Your church may very well feel good about its reception of LGBT people. But if you're looking not to go public with that information, the question you have to ask yourself is why does at least part of your denomination/congregation care about its posture with respect to gay people? Remember, 65% of mainliners care about this issue in general.

Presumably, some part of your church cares about welcoming gay people because they want gay people to feel welcome in church. No big mystery there. See, but here's the thing: If you don't make that fact public, how will gay people ever know they're welcome? If you don't ever publicly come out and say it, why do you think gay people will ever risk taking the time to find out?

The problem is that LGBT folks have traditionally found the church to be pretty uniformly hostile. Unless they see some extremely public sign that they're welcome, chances are, when they come upon your church, they're just going to keep walking. If you want gay people to come to your church, you're going to have to go out and wave some kind of rainbow colored flag to let them know it's safe to come inside. The burden isn't on them to do the spade work to find out if your church is a closeted Welcoming and Affirming congregation; the burden is on you. The point, of course, is that there are no "closeted" Welcoming and Affirming congregations.

A friend and gay colleague of mine once said to me that expecting gay people to show up at your church if you've failed to advertise it as safe for gay people is like expecting African-Americans to show up at a random hotel in rural areas of the South in 1966. Why would anyone risk that without some assurances?

"Maybe one of these days."

Let me go on record as saying that the acceptance of gay people into public life, and into the life of many churches (it will probably never be all churches), is inevitable at some point in the not-too-distant future. The statistics are pretty clear that the younger you are, the more likely you are not to have a problem, theological or otherwise, with LGBT people. As more and more young people take on positions of leadership and authority in society and in the church (and older ones exit the other side of the stage), this issue will cease to be an issue.

So, the welcoming of gay folks in church is a matter of *when*, not *if*. If you're already there but your church isn't, the question you need to ask yourself is about how a failure to act affects your LGBT brothers and sisters right now. Is history eventually going to vindicate them without the prophetic voice of the women and men God has called to lead the church? And if so, what kind of credibility will the church have forfeited when it becomes clear that the church once again let society do its heavy lifting?

"Well, that's fine for you. It's easy for you to sound all self-righteous. You're in a progressive church."

I'm not going to defend myself against that—although, I think I could. Instead, for the sake of discussion, I'll stipulate that you're right. I'm a self-righteous jerk. It's easy for me, and I never experience any difficulty over this issue, and grateful unicorns kiss the tip of my nose every night when I come home.

Now that that's out of the way, the question you still need to ask yourself is whether I'm telling the truth. Because if I'm telling the truth, all we're arguing about is whether or not you're going to do something about it.

Once again, I'll stipulate that it's difficult. It's hard, potentially-lose-your-job-and-your-friends kind of hard, lose-important-congregations-and-constituencies kind of hard. I know. I get it. But you're a minister of the gospel of Jesus Christ (whether or not you're ordained); hard is what you do—or, at least, it's what *he* did. I didn't make the map; I'm just telling you where I think it leads.

"I have to take the whole congregation into consideration ... not just those folks who agree with me."

On a theoretical level, I think I know what this means. Talking about taking the whole congregation into consideration, it is believed, is an attempt at fairness—sort of like the conversation every parent of multiple children eventually has:

"Dad, who's your favorite? Am I your favorite?"

"I'm a parent. You're *all* my favorites."

Whether or not it's possible for parents to avoid having favorites, the analogy falls apart when it comes to one very crucial issue: This issue isn't about liking one group of parishioners more than another or liking the liberals more than the conservatives—or even the *appearance* of liking one group more than another. This is an issue about faithfulness to what you understand to be the direction of God's reign in this world and your responsibility to point toward it.

"Meaning what, exactly? That sounds an awful lot like stacking the rhetorical deck in your favor."

Ah, yes. By this point we've established that I'm certainly not above stacking the rhetorical deck. Point taken.

Ok. Let me come at it a different way. If one of my children were to begin living in a way my wife and I were convinced was destructive, would the fact that another of my children pointed it out mean that I should ignore the destructive behavior—just so it didn't appear as though I favored one child over the other? Isn't there a sense in which keeping silent so as to avoid sibling rivalry ceases to be loving and becomes enabling? That is to say, isn't speaking truthfully a prerequisite to true love even being a possibility?

"But that's exceptionally patronizing, don't you think? It sounds like you're the parent and everyone else is a child—that you have all the answers, and that they can only hope to grow up spiritually with the benefit of your wise guidance."

Again, I hear you. However, I'm not sure it shakes out quite so easily as that. For one thing, pastors get paid to speak the truth; they don't get paid to keep the peace, if by peace you mean the maintenance of a theological DMZ. True peace is only possible where speaking the truth in love is a higher priority than preserving some mutually beneficial cease-fire.

Second, as a pastor, while I must retain a certain amount of humility about my capacity to have all the right answers, that doesn't mean that I should just shut up until we stumble across an issue upon which everybody already agrees. If the primary virtue of pastoral ministry centers on articulating non-controversial platitudes, there's really no need for pastors; all that's necessary is a "well-lubricated weather vane."

Note: If you're inclined, you can substitute "pastor" with "church leader." Same argument, since we're all ministers in virtue of our baptism.

Being prophetic is part of the job, though it can function as an altogether too-difficult-to-decline invitation to self-righteousness. I'm not saying it's easy; I'm just saying it's necessary.

"Once again. All that's easy for you to say. You don't face the same kind of pressures I face."

Perhaps not. I suspect I minister in a different environment than most people. But please don't be tempted to think that I operate in some blissful pastoral idyll. I still have to figure out which vocational hills are worth dying on—just like everybody else.

"Won't the 'losing' side be hurt ... perhaps enough to leave?"

What this question fails to take into account in a case like the exclusion of LGBT people from full participation in the life and ministry of the church is that there already is (and always has been) a "losing" side in this question; ignoring that reality is much easier, since historically minority groups have never had the power to make the cost-benefit analysis work in their favor.

In this case, concern about division has historically been calculated with the concerns of pro-exclusive forces as the determining factor (e.g., "If we accept these people, the 'anti' forces might leave."). Unfortunately, however, the church has already been voting on "winners" and "losers," but—it could be argued by the "losing" side—more on the basis of consequentialist calculations about which decision will make the fewest people angry, than on the basis of the theological integrity of the decision.

And, although it's a cliché to say it, *not* making a decision is making a decision.

"But won't welcoming LGBT people be divisive? Don't we have a responsibility to maintain unity?"

Welcoming LGBT people isn't divisive; it's the reality that such a display of hospitality seeks to overcome that is divisive. That people are excluded from participation in the life and ministry of the church because of their sexual orientation or gender identity, and that there are people who would champion this exclusion, is what is ultimately divisive.

Will it prompt some people and congregations to leave? If churches said openly that they welcome and affirm LGBT people, it might very well be given as the reason for some people and congregations to walk away from fellowship. Practically speaking, however, if mainline churches *don't* begin to claim their place as advocates on this issue, we also need to wonder just how many more people will leave what they take to be an unjust and exclusive denomination—and perhaps, just as importantly, how many people will never walk through the doors of a church that they consider unwelcoming?

"But what about our responsibility to preserve unity?"

Unity requires perseverance through the inevitable pain that comes with living in covenant with another. However, a unity achieved at the expense of what is right and true isn't unity at all—it's merely uniformity. That doesn't mean that we press every issue to the breaking point of our commitment to community. But it does mean that a unity that depends for its existence on the church looking past injustice is a unity that those people who love Jesus should have no investment in preserving.

A church (local, regional, or national) that regards the maintenance of unity as its highest priority is always in danger of misunderstanding unity as a *human achievement* rather than as a *divine gift*. In his great "high priestly prayer" in the Gospel of John, Jesus prayed "not only on behalf of" the disciples, "but also on behalf of those who will believe in me through their word, that they may all be one" (17:20-21a). The unity of the church on this account comes as a result of God's answer to Jesus' prayer, not because humans manage to muster up the stick-to-itiveness to avoid falling out over fundamental disagreements. The unity of the church is not ours to achieve; it is a reality with which Christians must align themselves. Either we swim with the current on this one, or we swim against it. What we *don't* do is create the current, then mandate its direction.

This emphasis on maintaining unity above virtually any other concern can lead to another potential pitfall: the mistaken belief that true unity can be present in the absence of true speech. Christian unity is not a consensual non-aggression pact that requires participants to refrain from speaking truthfully so as not to roil the ecclesiological waters.

"Yes, but we really don't want anybody to leave."

Conversations on whether or not a church should officially take on an identity that welcomes and affirms all people often seem to assume that only two groups have much interest in the fight—liberals and conservatives. Whatever decision you come to is guaranteed to make one side or another mad.

As a result, what savvy church leaders do is the utilitarian calculation about maximizing pleasure (in this case, pleasure can be defined as the absence of pain). Making decisions based on what will anger the fewest number of people seems to keep the waters calmer. Unfortunately, one group that gets left out of the calculation are those people who might be interested in church but who are scared away because of the perceived hostility to LGBT people. (In particular, if the statistics are correct, young people ... you know, the people all churches clamor after.)

"Why not consider people who are interested in the church, but who haven't yet come?"

For whatever reason, it's harder to take into consideration people who aren't seated around the decision-making table. From the church's standpoint, it's difficult to consider the impact of decision-making that excludes people who don't come anyway. You can't lose what you don't have, right? Bird in the hand, and all that.

I want to suggest, though, that this failure to factor into decision-making people who love the *idea* of Jesus—whom they understand to offer an expansive welcome to everyone, but whose followers often cultivate the perception that purity ranks infinitely higher on the list of priorities than hospitality—is one of the reasons young people are staying away from the church in droves.

As I've said, but it's worth repeating, according to research done a few years back by the Barna Group, an evangelical research firm, 91% of non-Christians age 16–29 believe that "anti-homosexual" is the term that best describes the church. Among church-going young people of the same age group, the number is only slightly better at 80% (http://www.barna.org/barna-update/article/16-teensnext-gen/94-a-new-generation-expresses-its-skepticism-and-frustration-with-christianity). (You get the mind-blowing significance of that, right? Even 8 out of 10 church-going young people—across the spectrum—think "hates gay people" when they hear the word "church.")

"Well, of course. The church has traditionally taken a position opposing homosexuality. So, that number may just be describing what everyone already considers the church's historic position on the issue, not the church's attitude toward gay people."

That might be an important objection, except that the Barna Group probed the perception and found that "non-Christians and Christians explained that beyond their recognition that Christians oppose homosexuality, they believe that Christians show excessive contempt and unloving attitudes towards gays and lesbians." The very group churches say they want to attract—declining mainline denominations in particular—have already formed strong opinions about the church's moral authority. That's increasingly problematic.

"Why?"

Again, according to Gallup, the truth of the matter is that "there is a gradual cultural shift under way in Americans' views toward gay individuals and gay rights." That shift is toward acceptance. Gallup indicates that "this year [2010], the shift is apparent in a record-high level of the public seeing gay and lesbian relations as morally acceptable." (http://www.gallup.com/poll/135764/Americans-Acceptance-Gay-Relations-Crosses-Threshold.aspx)

And the younger you are, the more likely it is that you believe that "gay and lesbian relations" are "morally acceptable."

"So, are you saying that the church should just follow the culture?"

No. I'm saying that if you *already* believe in the acceptance and celebration of folks who are LGBT but resist taking a public position on the issue for fear of alienating people, you need to realize that you're alienating more and more people every day by *not* taking that stance. As I said before, if you think the whole LGBT issue is wrong *tout court*, you probably stopped reading a long time ago—since my reflections are aimed at that already-convinced-but-not-ready-to-go-public segment of the church.

"Then, you're saying that the church should make theological decisions based on pragmatic considerations about church growth."

Again, no. If you've *already* made the theological determination that LGBT people deserve to be received with hospitality in the church but haven't made the decision to go public, all I'm saying is that refraining from taking a public position on the issue for fear that people will be alienated if you have the discussion, fails to take into account the fact that you're already alienating another group of people by *not* having the discussion—the very people (emerging generations) who every church and denomination I know of says they want.

Why not be just as afraid of losing people who aren't part of the church yet as of the people who might decide to leave? At least in the case of the latter, chances are extremely high that people who leave because you've decided to make this decision publicly will find a new church home. In the case of the former, however, chances are they'll never find a church home.

It's not easy.

Here's the thing: Our inability to speak out in favor of God's justice for LGBT folks comes with an opportunity cost.

"What do you mean by opportunity cost?"

Opportunity cost is the value of what you're willing to forgo by deciding to do one thing rather than another.

The question is: When will mainline denominations decide that the opportunity costs of inaction on the public acceptance of LGBT people are unacceptably high?

Make no mistake. The day is coming when full acceptance of LGBT people will be the norm in our society. But what mainline denominations must consider is whether they will have already driven so many people away that the victory will be too late. Because when the day comes that mainline denominations finally take that step, they're going to lose the people who won't change under any circumstances anyway. And the people who *had* been looking for a home may have already given up on the church—mainline or otherwise.

"We don't want to be known as a 'one-issue church'."

Put less diplomatically, as some people have done, the reservation is expressed this way:

"We don't want to be known as the 'gay church.'"

I want to address this matter because it can prove to be an obstacle for churches in entertaining the radical notion of becoming open and affirming.

This is worth talking about. The charge that focusing on LGBT inclusion carries with it the danger of consigning the church to a box reserved for single issue (and thus dismissible) matters marked "identity politics" (e.g., race, gender, ethnicity, etc.), misses a very important point.

"Open and Affirming"—or any of the other designations used to describe inclusive churches—is not simply code for "gay friendly." Because of the role I play as an advocate on this issue, I have been cautioned by more than a few people that O&A is seen by many to be a euphemism for militant gay friendliness.

"Urging churches to be O&A is a sure way to turn people off, because there's a long history behind that designation that many people hear as a call to become a 'gay church.'"

Ok. I get that, if by "Open and Affirming" what people mean is just another sneaky way to squeeze into the life of the church the "agenda-driven politics" of the LGBT community (perhaps a strawman argument all its own?). But the thing is: Nobody I know is making that argument.

Open and Affirming, Reconciling, More Light, Welcoming and Affirming—though they carry a specific and important association with the LGBT community—are about so much more than making churches "gay friendly"; they stand as various ways of calling the church to fundamentally reorient its understanding of hospitality and justice. The full inclusion of LGBT people only scratches the surface of the church's radical vocation to love those who've been kicked to the margins.

When a church becomes Open and Affirming, it soon finds that welcoming LGBT folks is just the beginning. Pretty soon, if you're serious about your faith, you begin to ask, "Who *else* has been left out that the church should be welcoming in? About who *else* has society generally said, 'You need not worry about *those* folks. We've got much more pressing concerns. Their stuff (even if we think they have a right to it, which oftentimes we do not) can wait.'"

Immigrants (legal and otherwise)? People of races different from mine? The poor? AIDS patients? Those who can't get health insurance? The disabled? Drug addicts? Ex-cons? Prostitutes and tax collectors? Lepers? You know, the disposable people.

Open and Affirming, after you live with it a while, instead of narrowing your focus to one beleaguered group, *broadens* your vision. It is a way of beginning to take seriously what otherwise gets so casually tossed about by popular Christianity: What would Jesus do?

Indeed, what *would* Jesus do? Which question is another way of asking, "Who would Jesus love? Who would Jesus welcome? Who would Jesus see cast off from the rest of 'normal' life, drop what he's doing with the highly accomplished and well situated, and go hang out with?"

Open and Affirming congregations, I want to suggest, are much less "single issue" churches than those congregations that spend the bulk of their time in extended instances of applied ecclesiological navel-gazing.

To the extent that a congregation/denomination spends the bulk of its time hand-wringing about its impending demise, for instance, it's a single issue church. Congregations that obsess about attracting young families, and denominations that obsess about attracting *anybody* are much closer to being single-issue churches than O&A congregations. You might just be a single-issue church if you spend more time talking about not having enough money than about what kinds of interesting things you're going to do with the money you've got. You get the idea.

The point is that becoming O&A doesn't limit the horizon of discipleship; in fact, it stretches it in revolutionary ways, offering a point of access to the radical hospitality and the institution-challenging justice practiced by Jesus himself. Perhaps discipleship, when all is said and done, *is* a single issue: Does the faith you practice assist you or prevent you from following Jesus into the parts of town where good Christian folks are often discouraged from going?

Field Notes

The world is changing faster than the church can keep up. In fact, the whole premise of this book is that the world has changed in ways that have profoundly perplexed that one-time cultural colossus: mainline Protestantism.

In the case of the acceptance of homosexuality, however, mainline Protestantism (at least a sizable majority) has changed along with the rest of the cultural mainstream. Unfortunately, because mainliners have often been unwilling to say otherwise, emerging generations lump mainliners together with all other Christians in that category known as antihomosexual. Confronting the prospect of a post-denominational world ought to prompt mainline denominations to take seriously their relationship to those people who've been cast aside because of sexual orientation or gender identity. And by "take seriously" I mean "repair."

I realize repairing the relationship between the church and the LGBT community poses a great challenge. LGBT people have suffered a lot, much of it at the hands of the church. This suffering has sometimes come as a result of outright violence in word and deed and, perhaps just as damaging, through silence in the face of such injustice. Consequently, the damage will be difficult to repair. But repair it we must.

Many people, especially emerging generations, view discrimination against LGBT folks as the most important civil rights issue of our day. Again, you may not agree with that sentiment. However, what you need to pay attention to is the fact that an increasing majority of Americans think it's the case. And if you want to remain in conversation (especially with young people), you need to be aware that they see *you* as the arterial plaque in the body politic when it comes to this issue. And even if tomorrow every mainline denomination, along with all their congregations, should declare themselves More Light, Reconciling, Open or Welcoming and Affirming, an enormous amount of fence mending would still need to happen. You can't just go stand on the front steps and yell: "Okay, gay people, it's safe to come in now!"

Here, even if tomorrow every mainline denomination says: "A lot of LGBT people grew up in the church. And though many of them suffered unspeakable damage, which caused them to leave the church, not all of them gave up on God." There are significant numbers of LGBT folks (and the people who love them) who'd like to come back to church, but they're understandably scared. Who wouldn't be?

What Can You Do?

- Put something on your church sign and on the home page of your website indicating that LGBT people are safe with you. Your declaration needs to be public and unambiguous, or chances are pretty good they won't risk it.

- Consider starting (and participating in) a PFLAG (Parents, Families and Friends of Lesbians and Gays) chapter.

- Get in touch with LGBT advocacy and support groups and volunteer (e.g., volunteer the use of your van, your building for meetings, your copy machine, your people to staff booths). This takes an investment of time, since gaining trust often requires you to work on establishing relationships. That means that you often have to show up at things (e.g., meetings, promotional events, lobby days, parades, etc.) for which you have no responsibility.

- Follow and "like" those advocacy and support groups on social media. Simple to do, but it makes an impact when people are checking you out if they see you're willing to offer public support.

- See if there's any energy in your community around issues that need advocacy (e.g., hate crimes legislation, fair housing/employment/ public accommodations legislation, anti-bullying legislation, marriage equality, adoption, etc.). Then, lend your voice.

- Consider having your (willing) young people trained as peer counselors for LGBT youth who are dealing with issues around coming out or bullying or just plain growing up.

- Pass a resolution telling the world your denomination welcomes and affirms everyone into full participation in the life and ministry of the church. I know, resolutions don't do anything. Actually, that's not entirely true. Resolutions do communicate to the world who you, at your best, desire to be. Resolutions aren't necessarily indicative; they can be subjunctive. That is to say, they need not be descriptive of the "conditions on the ground"; they can be aspirational about a world you envision.

Conclusion

I began this book in the ancient mountains of Appalachia, where the ravages of decline from the coal industry are stark. As I conclude, I turn to the drought-ravaged mountains of central Mexico. Perspective on the world comes more naturally from the heights of mountains. Therefore, mountains seem a good metaphor for the search for perspective I have tried to provide.

I am in Mexico as I write this. I can see the sun at work drying the hard brown earth. Children playing soccer make dust devils swirl as they run.

San Luis Potosí lies nestled in the arid mountains of central Mexico. It's difficult to imagine that anything can grow here, since so much of the year passes without rain. Yet everywhere you look you can see small patches of green fingers poking out from the ground—a little grass here and there, cacti, mesquite trees. The bougainvilleas paint purple and red pictures against a brown backdrop.

Walking out in the countryside, however, emphasizes the inhospitable nature of the environment. Rocks, sand, mountains—at times an almost lunar landscape. Beauty, but a dread kind of beauty—angular, lots of sharp barbs and keen edges.

As I walk, I puzzle over who it was that wandered into this part of the world first and thought it might make a good home. Water is a mission rather than a natural resource. Food requires imagination and ingenuity borne on the bent back of sun-scorched labor.

And yet, in the midst of this uncooperative terrain, life blooms. Stubborn plants prosper. Animals breed. People live and love and create; they produce children who laugh and old people who still sing. "How can this be?" I wonder. In conditions less than hospitable to life, life flourishes. Sinuous. Unyielding. Spiny. It makes no sense that I can see. Still there is life.

People have speculated about the viability of Christianity. In particular, the church and its waning popularity have stood at the center of the discussion. The numbers seem clear: The church, with few exceptions, has fallen on hard times. The soil that only a few generations ago was fertile and black has hardened—just a few unflagging tendrils peeking through cracks, a flash of color here and there from plants that will not surrender, a tree or a cactus that has made peace with its grim environment.

But there is life ... and if you look closely, more life than first meets the eye. There are churches thriving under impossible circumstances: announcing the reign of God, pursuing justice, tending the sick, feeding the hungry, holding hands with those left to die in the desert.

It occurs to me that the church has experienced lean seasons in the past. But every time things green up for a bit, we think the fat years are permanent, that the land of milk and honey knows no drought or blight. But plenty never lasts. On the other hand, neither does lean.

What an inhospitable environment *can* produce is strength and focus, and the tenacity to do what we have been given to do, even though we may never see it result in the kind of fecundity we think signals "success."

Heroes and saints are almost never made during easy times. The first holy mothers and fathers bloomed in the desert, after all.

Heroes and saints aren't people who do great things for God because they have no shortcomings, no flaws, no challenges from their environment; heroes and saints are people who do great things for God in spite of the fact that the deck's stacked against them, that the shortcomings and flaws always threaten to undo them, that the environment in which they live doesn't want them. Heroes and saints are people determined to live their everyday lives as if God matters more than the sum total of their weaknesses and challenges.

Mainline denominations may very well be in the desert.

Now, I think, is the time for heroes and saints, for a church unwilling to yield. For we may live in a post-denominational world—a world in which denominational decline signals the death of institutions and ways of doing things that only a few short years ago seemed triumphant and inevitable.

What I have tried to do in this book is to provide hope that even should mainline denominations and many of their congregations die, the work of God's reign will continue on new frontiers. It has survived deadly drought before, and it will continue to survive.

I believe that mainline denominations, if they resist the urge to fall into despair, can survive the desert, can escape the vortex of doom, which threatens to suck the life out of the church. Mainline denominations, which inhabit the grace-filled, ecumenical, expansive vision of God's work, need to find and empower those pioneers who would once again venture into unknown territories to do God's work.

Bibliography

Ahlstrom, Sydney E. *A Religious History of the American People.* 2nd ed. New Haven, Conn.: Yale University Press, 2004.

Berry, Wendell. *What Are People For?* New York: North Point Press, 1990.

Boring, M. Eugene. *Disciples and the Bible: A History of Disciples Biblical Interpretation in North America.* St. Louis: Chalice Press, 1997.

Bose, Adrija. "Social Media in Tahrir Square: How Freemona Resulted in Freeing Mona." *First World Post.* 2011.http://www.firstpost.com/world/social-media-intahir-square-how-resulted-in-freeing-mona-209032.html.

Carlson, Peter. "The Bible According to Thomas Jefferson." *American History.* October, 2011.

Cowles, Joshua. "The Internet as Utopia: Reality, Virtuality, and Politics." *Oshkosh Scholar* IV (2009): 81–89. Finke, Roger, and Rodney Stark. *The Churching of America, 1776-2005: Winners and Losers in Our Religious Economy.* New Brunswick, N.J.: Rutgers University Press, 2005.

Fox, Richard Wrightman. Jefferson, Emerson, and Jesus. *Raritan* 22.1 (2002): 62–78.

Gannes, Liz. "Does Social Media Help Foment Revolution? A Theory from within Twitter." Allthingsd.com. March 18, 2011.

Garrison, W.E., and A.T. DeGroot. *The Disciples of Christ. A History.* St. Louis: The Bethany Press, 1969.

Goodale, Gloria. "In Libya, Perfecting the Art of Revolution by Twitter." *The Christian Science Monitor.* May 10, 2011.

Handy, Robert T. *A History of the Churches in the United States and Canada.* New York: Oxford University Press, 1977.

Hatch, Nathan O. *The Democratization of American Christianity.* New Haven: Yale University Press, 1989.

Isaacson, Walter. 2011. *Steve Jobs.* New York: Simon and Schuster.

Kant, Immanuel. "What Is Enlightenment?" in *On History.* Ed. Lewis White Beck. Indianapolis,: Bobbs-Merrill, 1963.

Kinnaman, David, and Gabe Lyons. *Unchristian: What a New Generation Really Thinks About Christianity...And Why It Matters.* Grand Rapids: Baker Books, 2007.

Langley, David and van den Broek, Tijs, http://microsites.oii.ox.ac.uk/ipp2010/system/files/IPP2010_Langley_vandenBroek_Paper.pdf, September 16–17 2010).

Lord, Joseph, Alex Orlando, and James Bruggers. "Excessive Heat; Triple Digit Records Falling with Regularity in Louisville," *The Courier Journal.* July 16, 2012.

McAllister, Lester G., and William Tucker. *Journey in Faith: A History of the Christian Church (Disciples of Christ).* St. Louis: Chalice Press, 1975.

Noll, Mark A. *A History of Christianity in the United States and Canada.* Grand Rapids, Mich.: W.B. Eerdmans, 1992.

Oduor, Atieno, et al. "Grandparents Caring for Their Grandchildren: Emerging Roles and Exchanges in Global Perspectives." *Journal of Comparative Family Studies* 40. (September 2009): 827–48.

Pressfield, Stephen. *The War of* Art. New York: Black Irish Entertainment LLC, 2002.

Sachs, Jeffery. *The End of Poverty: Economic Possibilities for Our Time.* Reprint ed. New York: Penguin Books, 2006.

Shermer, Michael. *How We Believe: Science, Skepticism, and the Search for God.* 2nd Ed. New York: Holt Books, 2003.

Smith, Christian, and Patricia Snell. *Souls in Transition : The Religious and Spiritual Lives of Emerging Adults.* Oxford: New York: Oxford University Press, 2009.

Stone, Barton. *History of the Christian Church in the West.* Lexington, K.Y.: College of the Bible, 1956.

Stone, Barton, and John Rogers. *The Biography of Eld. Barton Warren Stone.* Cincinnati: J.A. & U.P. James, 1847.

Toulouse, Mark G. *Joined in Discipleship: The Shaping of Contemporary Disciples Identity.* St. Louis: Chalice Press, 1997.

Willimon, William, and Stanley Hauerwas, *Resident Aliens: Life in the Christian Colony.* Nashville: Abingdon Press, 1989.